her Savior and the life found in the freedom of His love. With uncanny wisdom, insight, and unbelievable depth, Rita has offered an incredible book that, if heeded and lived, will change your life, your personal perspectives, and your view of God's unending love. Devour, soak, and trust the truths of *Finding Eve* and find the real you that you were created to be.

—THOMAS AND MARY BETH MILLER
WORSHIP PASTORS, GATEWAY CHURCH
DALLAS, TEXAS

Rita Springer has been a true mentor to me for fifteen years now via her music, and in more recent years as true sisters and friends. Her responses to life and love have tutored me. I am delighted to see her worship and heart now poured out in black and white in the pages of *Finding Eve*. In such an inspired and creative way, Rita brings to life the possible musings of Eve's heart and gives us insight into our own. Enjoy this journey.

—JENNIE LEE RIDDLE
DOVE AWARD—WINNING SONGWRITER OF "REVELATION SONG"
AND "HOPE OF THE BROKEN WORLD"

Rita is a treasured member of our team at Gateway, and we're thrilled for you to receive the wisdom she imparts in *Finding Eve*. Her unique voice carries an unending passion for God's presence and a deep desire for others to find their freedom in His love. By living a life dedicated and devoted to the Lover of her soul, Rita has found His answer to the longing of every woman's soul.

—ROBERT AND DEBBIE MORRIS
PASTORS, GATEWAY CHURCH
BEST-SELLING AUTHORS OF *THE BLESSED LIFE*, *THE BLESSED MARRIAGE*, *THE BLESSED WOMAN*, *FROM DREAM TO DESTINY*, AND *THE GOD I NEVER KNEW*

I so admire and respect Rita's relentless passion for Jesus! Her writing is infused with worship and consistently leads me toward the throne of our Creator Redeemer.

—LISA HARPER
AUTHOR, BIBLE TEACHER, AND SPEAKER FOR
WOMEN OF FAITH CONFERENCES

So much of our understanding of who we are as believers stems from belief systems that go back to the very beginning. Rita's heart to unpack some of these beliefs sheds light on how to become fully free in our calling and life in and before God. I've known Rita for many years and have watched her unfold into one who is passionately in love with the One she's given all for. Her sharing, her songs, and now this book can only reveal the journey of one abandoned to the highest call of intimacy. Rita's heart for women has always been to see them become free in worship and therefore in all of life. I believe this book can be helpful for all to discover the promises of God and how to walk in the fullness and hope of what it looks like to be abandoned and therefore free in Him.

—CHRISTY WIMBER
SENIOR LEADER, YORBA LINDA VINEYARD AND
YORBA LINDA VINEYARD RESOURCE CENTER

Finding Eve is incredible. Rita has been a mentor in my life for many years. She has an anointing to speak the absolute truth in love and to be transparent about your pain and insecurities. This beautiful book will help you find Him as you examine your own heart. You will be changed.

—Kari Jobe
Worship Leader and Recording Artist

Rita Springer has written a book that will take every woman on a journey of healing and hope as they find God's true plan for them as His daughters. Rita's heart to serve people out of passionate love for God comes through loud and clear in *Finding Eve*. I recommend it as a resource for all the women in your life!

—Tom Lane
Executive Senior Pastor, Gateway Church
Dallas, Texas

Wow, wow, wow! From the very beginning of this book I was pulled into a vacuum of God's presence, and there the Holy Spirit took His gentle finger to uproot those destructive weeds in the garden of my heart that caused me to doubt my value and self-worth. Look out, weeds—be prepared to be uprooted. This book is a spiritual "weedwacker"! A must-read for every woman who must find her true identity! Bravo, Rita, bravo!

—Maria Durso
Copastor, Christ Tabernacle Church
Glendale, New York

Wow! Women all over the world need this book now! Having been personal friends with Rita for more than a decade, we have witnessed firsthand the life of a godly woman who has uncompromisingly dedicated herself to the passionate pursuit of

finding
eve

finding
eve

Discover your true identity as a
DAUGHTER OF GOD

RITA SPRINGER

Most CHARISMA HOUSE BOOK GROUP products are available at special quantity discounts for bulk purchase for sales promotions, premiums, fund-raising, and educational needs. For details, write Charisma House Book Group, 600 Rinehart Road, Lake Mary, Florida 32746, or telephone (407) 333-0600.

FINDING EVE by Rita Springer
Published by Passio
Charisma Media/Charisma House Book Group
600 Rinehart Road
Lake Mary, Florida 32746
www.charismahouse.com

Library of Congress Control Number: 2013903000
International Standard Book Number: 978-1-62136-050-6
E-book ISBN: 978-1-62136-204-3

While the author has made every effort to provide accurate
telephone numbers and Internet addresses at the time of
publication, neither the publisher nor the author assumes
any responsibility for errors or for changes that occur after
publication.

AUTHOR'S NOTE: Some names, places, and identifying
details with regard to stories in this book have been changed
to help protect the privacy of individuals who may have had
similar experiences. The illustrations may consist of composites
of a number of people with similar issues and names and
circumstances changed to protect their confidentiality. Any
similarity between the names and stories of individuals
described in this book to individuals known to readers is purely
coincidental.

First edition

13 14 15 16 17 — 9 8 7 6 5 4 3 2 1
Printed in the United States of America

I dedicate this book to my beautiful mother, Juanita May Springer. She left this world a long time ago, but every tear she shed and prayer she prayed went down deep, took root, and shaped itself in this heart of mine. What a legacy of belief she left me. I am without words at the thought that out of all of the mothers in the entire world, she was my mom. She was the best mother I could have had, and she did an excellent job pointing me toward the Savior. I wrote this book to honor her legacy and influence others, because I had her to influence me.

To every Eve in every city in every nation, follow the voice of the One who will lead you back into gardens of life and freedom, and whose grace will always give you hope.

CONTENTS

ACKNOWLEDGMENTS

I WANT TO THANK first Adrienne Gaines at Charisma House for being curious enough after just seeing the title *Finding Eve* to want to know more. Thank you, Adrienne, for all your hard work and encouragement to see this come out of me in the way it needed to.

Thank you to Pastor Robert and Debbie Morris, Thomas Miller, and Pastor Tom Lane at Gateway Church for believing enough in me to encourage me to dream again.

I want to thank the Eves in my life who have shown me true friendship and loved and prayed me whole: Kim Aube, Michele Benson, Laura Lee, Leisa Nelson, Paula Antonelli, Lindsay Huckins, Jennie Riddle, and Christy Wimber.

I want to acknowledge and thank my sisters, who are all strong and courageous daughters of Eve: Roxanne Boonstra, Cathleen Springer, Laurie Sherwood, Linda

Springer, Kristy Springer, and Debbie Springer. I love how different you all are, and I love being your sister.

To Tiffany Jones and Amanda Boonstra and all my DIVE students, you are the next generation of Eves. I am in the balcony cheering you all on.

To my Justice—I love you deeply, son. Thank you for letting all these words be written while you played with cars, built LEGOs, flew toy airplanes, and read stories curled up next to me, falling asleep to the clicking of the keyboard. You are God's gift to me, and I love being your mother.

FOREWORD

L OOKING ACROSS THE pages of my life, I see a trail of highlighted marks—moments of significance that propelled me into my future. Largely they've come through the encouragement of others, sometimes tucked away in conversations that opened my heart and mind; but other times they came from words on a page or songs I heard, where someone I did not personally know spoke into my desert places, making a profound impact.

I started listening to Rita's worship music as a teen and was immediately drawn to the authenticity that flowed through her melodies and into the deep recesses of my heart. Her life-giving lyrics resonated and brought release when I least expected but most needed it. Without realizing it, Rita became my friend and encourager, instigating a deeper inward hunger and greater outward reach, leading to growth, which would be vital in the coming days.

Our first meeting was at a Vineyard Worship Conference in the fall of 1999. My dad was walking with my infant daughter in the aisle, and Rita stopped to talk with him and pray over Abigail. Without our exchanging words, a tangible connection was formed. It built upon the framework of many years in which her songs had carried me through suffocating sorrow, helped me celebrate moments of exuberant joy, and peacefully filled the quiet spaces in between.

In the weeks following the Amish schoolhouse shooting, where my then husband took the lives of five girls before taking his own, one of Rita's songs often rang throughout our home. The lyrics of her song "I Want the Joy" changed our atmosphere. I wanted the joy of the Lord to fall down, to be in my life, to lift me and change me, just as Rita sang. There was no way to sing the lyrics and not experience transforming joy. Rita was again present in my places of brokenness, releasing hope over my family.

In April 2008 I went to her website looking for some new music to download and realized she was coming to a town nearby to lead a conference. At the prompting of the Lord, I sent an e-mail expressing that while I didn't know what her life looked like, I had been blessed because she allowed her experiences to lead her into deep places of worship and abandon. She helped me worship through my brokenness, and I was lifted, strengthened, and healed—propelled into deeper belief in a loving God. I told her she had mentored me from far away, without ever knowing it. I ended up going to the conference, and at the end Rita and her team spent time praying over me. Chains fell off, and I was set free from pain that had encased me following Charlie's destructive decisions.

That summer I attended Rita's DIVE school (diveworship .com), where I found the freedom to dream again. God's promises over my life were stirred, and I reached further than I'd ever thought possible. I began to see myself differently and recognize treasures buried deep within. DIVE unlocked the writer in me, a catalyst for the amazing God-journey I've been on ever since!

Finding Eve, much like the DIVE school, was birthed in Rita's heart as she talked with Jesus. He's unfolded deep revelation to her, which she now shares through conferences, mentoring, and within this book. As you turn the pages, you will find something greater than her story—you will find yourself. *Your* struggles are outlined; *your* passionate heartbeat heard; *your* soul bared before God. *Finding Eve* is not about the finger-pointing choices that destroyed intimacy for the human race. *Finding Eve* is about redemption. It's an invitation to come before the throne of God in nakedness, hiding nothing, willing to be seen and choosing to see yourself through His eyes of love.

Each of us has been Eve, sinking our teeth into the lie that we can't possibly be the habitation of Almighty God. Sometimes it feels easier to listen to the enemy and swallow the lie of unworthiness. But that's *not* our identity. God sees the destiny and speaks promise and redemption over us.

Admitting you have failed does not make you a failure. Let God show you what He sees. Trust His voice and embrace the love He extends. Right now He is declaring His love over you. He shouts in whispers only your heart can hear. He dances with revelry only your spirit can feel. And He's weaving threads of love into warmth that covers and thaws the once frozen places within. Dare to dream and believe He has more for you than what you see right now. Reach for the beauty within and follow where He leads. Your future is limitless, because His love knows no bounds.

Come with Rita as she leads you through this journey. Listen to the voice of a spiritual sister and mother, receiving the encouragement and friendship she offers. This is not about getting to a destination; it's about embracing the journey. You will find more of yourself with every step. You are strong; you are beautiful; you house the King—you are enough. It's time. This is your season; the day of advance is upon you—take back what the enemy has stolen.

—MARIE MONVILLE
AUTHOR OF *ONE LIGHT STILL SHINES*

INTRODUCTION

For more than fifteen years I have had the honor of leading and teaching worship all over the world. Many of those events have been women's conferences, and through the years I noticed a common thread of need among the women who came to the altar for prayer. I saw so many women suffering from shame, self-loathing, and self-discrimination it was staggering. The pattern was just too obvious to ignore.

I knew from personal experience that at the root of those feelings were insecurity and inferiority. Because those issues had never been dealt with, they were now wreaking havoc in these women's lives. The stories were all different, with some more traumatic and devastating than others, but the root was the same.

My heart would break for these precious ladies, especially

when I saw how they responded whenever I sang or spoke about my own struggles with insecurity and shame and how God set me free. When the women heard my story, it seemed to give them permission to finally start admitting what was really at the root of the burdens they were carrying.

I wanted to help women discover hope that would last a lifetime, not just for a few moments at the altar. It was clear to me that something was missing in the way we encouraged one another as women. But more seriously I saw that we lacked true understanding of why we were made and who formed us. I felt that knowing those truths was the key to healing all the places that were aching in these women's hearts.

I did not set out to find all the answers, but I wanted to see if God had something to say about the kinds of lies we as women were believing to have lost sight of how much God values us. I had been changed myself when I received the revelation of God's opinion of me, and I wanted others to discover the same truth.

Because sin was birthed through a lie, I was led right back to the garden and to the first woman who listened to the wrong voice. I began searching for Eve, not to put her mistakes under a microscope but to trace the effects of shame and insecurity all the way back to their root.

I knew little about Eve outside of her few short appearances in Scripture, where her name is mentioned only four times in the Bible. My opinion of Eve had been shaped by conventional teachings that presented her as too weak to resist temptation and simply a counterpart to Adam. I had failed to see her as anything more than an afterthought, God's response to Adam's need for companionship.

In many ways I had given her as much value as I had given myself before I sought God for help and healing. My opinion of myself changed when I began asking God what He thought about me. So I started asking God what His thoughts were about Eve. He answered by leading me to connect several dots in Scripture and see some precious life lessons in her story that hold beautiful truths for all women.

I began to identify with Eve as a woman who had been handcrafted by God with grand intention but who, after making some mistakes, had to fight hard to believe that. Eve was our beginning as women, and in her story she left a trail of revelation for us to learn and gain strength from. My challenge was to write about her without having many biblical and historical resources to glean from. Little has been written about Eve. How would I take those four mentions in Scripture and write all I felt led of the Holy Spirit to say?

My desire was to paint a picture of Eve that would help encourage women today in dealing with the real-life issues they face. I thought, "Why not begin each chapter with a journal selection from Eve?", as if such a document had been found. I was not sure how to pull it off, but I journal avidly and loved the prospect of imagining what Eve may have felt and thought at pivotal moments in her life. It would be fictional, of course, because we don't know what life was like for Eve, much less how she felt. But even if not perfectly accurate, Eve's journal entries would finally make her real and show women the similarities between her experiences and ours.

Helping women relate to Eve was most important to me, because her journey to rediscover her worth is so much like our own. Eve is not a confusing character, but her actions confused the intentions of God's destiny over her life. She is a product of what self-doubt and self-reliance can do to a soul that has been intentionally designed and created with purpose.

Like us, Eve was perfectly made. Just as we were knit together in our mother's wombs, our loving Creator formed Eve with His own hands. Yet a costly mistake caused her to lose the perfect life she had known and forced her into an unfamiliar world marked by pain and difficulty. Her sense of identity had to have been shaken. She went from having dominion with Adam over everything in Eden, with her every need met by her loving Maker, to submissively supporting her husband as he worked the soil to provide for his family.

After she and Adam were expelled from Eden, I imagine she felt shame, guilt, loss, disappointment with her circumstances, and possibly even apprehension about the future. She no longer enjoyed the same level of intimacy with the Father. She desired—dare I say, *needed*—her husband in a way she never had before. Then the children came. She was wife. She was mother. But who was *Eve* now? Was she still loved? Was she still cherished? Did she still have value, and if so, where did that sense of worth come from?

How many of us feel like we're not living the life we were meant to have? How many of us get lost beneath the responsibilities of marriage, motherhood, and careers? How many of us wonder what makes us valuable, if God still sees us in our pain, if He still has a plan after our failures?

The more I studied and listened to God talk about His firstborn daughter, the more I realized there was enough revelation about her to encourage her gender in the struggle to get back to the garden, which is the heart of God. It was there that Eve discovered how precious she was to the Father, how vital she was to His plan, and how closely He held her to His heart, even in those times when she felt most alone. By finding Eve, we too can find our way to that place of security and hope.

So much of my own healing from disappointment, failings, and feelings of inadequacy came with the revelations God gave me when I risked asking what His thoughts were about me. He showed me how much I meant to Him and what He desires for me. And He took me back to the root of the struggle for worth and identity that I had been locked in. Eve's story was, for me, a huge flashing red light to stop and take notice of how far back those feelings of being less than go.

Women were not created to be inferior and were never meant to feel that way. That insecurity is deeply rooted in our lineage. That lineage began with a young bride in a place called Eden.

With a hope and a heart to see His kingdom advance, God grabbed a rib and began to build a dream. I was knit with the same love, and I came from that same dreaming, as did every other woman after Eve. In finding Eve, I found her Maker, who despite my mistakes was still holding on to every hope and every plan He ever designed for me to accomplish. With God all things are possible. I am certain this is true for you as well.

Join me as I follow Eve's journey to discover her true identity as a daughter of God. My hope is that as you read this book, you will finally see the true name tag on your spirit, and that God will take you back to the garden gates and tell you that even though your life isn't going as planned, He still has one. Be encouraged.

No matter what life has thrown our way, no matter what mistakes we've made, you and I are still Eves who have been redeemed by God. We have been set apart to see and advance His great kingdom.

1
FINDING *an* EDUCATION

I am Eve. That is my name. I was brought into this world a short time ago, formed in a way no other will ever be—through the rib of my counterpart, Adam. Yes, a rib! Everything else about me came from the mind of Yahweh. He is the Maker and Creator of all we see. He also created Adam and myself. We are both unique and different, crafted with intention and wisdom. He loves us more than we can understand, and He says He will show us all things.

Language and understanding came quickly to us. I walk with Yahweh in the east part of the garden, which He calls the Secret Place, and He shows me all His voice called into being. Creation was complete in less than seven days! I stand and listen to the sound of creation's worship being carried along in the breeze right into Yahweh's heart. It is glorious to hear every living, breathing thing in Eden giving its praise to God, honoring Him continuously with their endless chorus of thankfulness.

Adam and I are here together in Yahweh God's paradise. We are His breath, His hand, His life poured into every part of our being. I know my purpose. It is to bring honor to God, to live in complete abandon, and to know and be known by this great God.

I am the only one here made like me. Adam is called male, and I am female. Yahweh says I was made with "intent" and "ability." He says I shall be able to do wonderful things, and that I alone have the ability to cradle life. I listen with curiosity. What will this all look like? I am full of information. I am full of excitement.

Yahweh tells us to eat when we are hungry and to sleep when we need rest. He speaks of day and night, and teaches us how to respect and honor this place. He gives us all we need. He tells us to taste and see His goodness over us. We govern here, Adam and me, side by side—man and woman, made in the image of God.

All we see we can have. Yet there is a tree—one tree—that is different. Yahweh says the fruit on that tree must never be eaten. He says our eyes would be opened if we ate of it, and we would die. We do not know what this death means, but without question we believe.

The strange creature took me by surprise. He spoke words that bruised my spirit. He questioned me about my place in God's heart. He asked me many things, and I was not sure of the answers. I was certain Yahweh had spoken of these things, but he asked in such a way that I questioned what I knew. I should have never entered into a conversation with him, but I did. My first mistake was that I answered him back. I should have taken his questions back to God, but I did not. He told me I was beautiful and lovely. He admired my hair and the color of my eyes. He asked me if I knew I was beautiful. Yahweh had said I was made perfect, but was I beautiful? This serpent made me nervous.

I looked for Adam. I almost called for him to come but felt provoked to defend myself. When I found Adam later, it was not to share with him my strength but to share my compromise. The serpent had asked me about the forbidden tree and its fruit. "Did God really tell you to not eat that?" he hissed. Yahweh said we could have anything in the field of living, but we were to stay away from the fruit of that center tree. The creature told me I did not know God like he did, that we would not die as Yahweh had said. I listened and became his fool. My flesh held fast to what I would come to understand was a lie.

I had never been lied to before that day. That is not to make excuses, but at the time the serpent brought great confusion to me. I was curious to know why this creature spoke so harshly of God, who could only have been his Creator as well. I stayed to listen when I should have run away.

The pressure I felt in those moments constrained me. The confusion that surrounded me was paralyzing—all because I entertained a stranger's voice. My choice changed life as I knew it. Creation seemed to warn me with its groaning, but still I disobeyed. I doubted my way with Yahweh. I put His word on trial and rejected its truth with my actions. I bit into the lie thinking I would be like God. Yet the moment I disobeyed I somehow knew that I had just placed myself on the outside of everything I was made for. I had all I needed in the garden, and I let a ground crawler harass me. I chose its truth because I allowed myself to think I was lacking something. I swayed Adam with my decision. I led him into my darkness, not realizing my misery wanted company.

We were ashamed. We were shivering. We were appalled at what we had done. We ran hiding from God. A sudden fear that we were unprotected and exposed haunted us. Our flesh now exposed and wretched, we heard God call for us. I huddled in shame with Adam as Yahweh held out His hand, beckoning us to run to Him. We could not. We felt at odds with God and with each other. Blame tossed itself into our reality. Adam pointed to me, and I pointed to the serpent. No longer would Adam and I hear each other's hearts like melodies together with harmonies. In that moment we became separate in thought and struggled for the sweet sound of communion. God, seeing our wrong, sentenced *us to what we did not understand, confusion now causing us to defend ourselves against His authority.*

I had been handcrafted by Yahweh and asked to believe I was fearfully and wonderfully made. Yet I lost my wisdom trying to steal what belonged to Him. I lost my innocence trying to define it, and I lost my peace and became acquainted with fear. That day I lost my identity. I am now in search of it again . . .

IN THE BEGINNING . . .

And no shrub of the field had yet appeared on the earth and no plant of the field had yet sprung up, for the LORD God had not sent rain on the earth and there was no man to work the ground, but streams came up from the earth and watered the whole surface of the ground—the LORD God formed the man from the dust of the ground and breathed into his nostrils the breath of life, and the man became a living being. Now the LORD God had planted a garden in the east, in Eden; and there he put the man he had formed. And the LORD God made all kinds of trees grow out of the ground—trees that were pleasing to the eye and good for food. In the middle of the garden were the tree of life and the tree of the knowledge of good and evil.

—GENESIS 2:5–9

Eve was not an educated woman by today's standards. There were no universities for her to attend, no degrees for her to earn, no intellectual heights for her to achieve. But that doesn't mean Eve didn't get an education. In the brief time we spend with her in Scripture, it is clear that Eve learned a great many things.

Eve had no reason to worry about her gifts, talents, abilities, and destiny. She was the first, made in perfection, and therefore faced no competition. When the Father fashioned her and gave her breath, He provided her with all she would ever need. Yet with all the gifts she was given—intelligence and beauty, wisdom and influence—Eve, like Adam, was also given the ability to choose. So when a snake told her God's word could not be trusted—that she wouldn't *really* die if she ate of the forbidden tree—she made a choice to doubt. And with that decision she lost not only the keys to her perfection but also a piece of her inheritance.

I believe Eve to have been a simple, organic girl whose weakness—her inclination to doubt herself and God—would cause her to seek strength from her relationships with God, Adam, and the sons and daughters who would come later. After all, she was not only created because her presence pleased God—she was also created for relationship.

It might seem that Eve's life was too different from ours for us to compare her plight with ours. We may think, "If Eve, who was created in a world without human sin and lived in paradise, would choose to believe a lie, what hope do we have?" There is so much more darkness around us, the strength it takes today to avoid doubting God's love and goodness makes Eve's life seem easy. Yet if that is the case, if it takes so much more strength to follow God today than it did in the garden, how much more strength and peace will we find when we do the hard work to overcome the darkness attempting to invade our lives?

The truth is, we are not so much different from Eve. If we were willing to turn the lights on in all the rooms of our lives, we would find the same fears, the same worries, the same longings and insecurities. So many of us, like Eve, fail to truly know our worth. We too fall victim to Satan's lies. But there is great freedom awaiting those of us who take notice of the "uneducated Eve" in our own hearts and educate her.

Eve is every size and shape, every color and race. She is the city girl and the country girl. She is all suburban and all urban and modern. She is young, and she is old. She is the remake, rebirth, and ongoing handiwork of the creative God who sketched out the very first Eve, knowing the names of every Eve who would come after her.

There is so much for us to learn from Eve. She discovered weakness in wonder and resentment in a decision that led her to stray. She learned regret in a moment and experienced heartbreak for a lifetime. Most of us can say the very same thing about our own lives. We learn from our mistakes. We can also learn from Eve's.

Eve is our professor; we are her students. Her life shows us what is birthed when we make a decision to doubt. The choice she faced in the garden was unavoidable, but doubting was optional. Eve became a shadow of what was to come, and her legacy speaks volumes into our futures. What can be gained if we value God enough to let Him come and invade our space, to let Him tell us more about why the tree of the knowledge of good and evil was not healthy to touch? These are the lessons Eve can teach us.

Eve steps into her first mistake in Genesis 3 when she decides to have a conversation with God's enemy. Satan poses a question that causes Eve to doubt her Maker. *"Did God really say?"* Satan begins (Gen. 3:1). It is here in her beginning that Eve falls prey to the tactic the enemy would use to attack women throughout history and even today. If we begin to question truth, we fall victim to the lie. Scripture says, "When the woman saw that the fruit of the tree was good for food and pleasing to the eye, and also desirable for gaining wisdom, she took some and ate it" (Gen. 3:6). It is here that I think Eve made the great mistake, and the temptation she faced is one we as women still are challenged with constantly.

Eve was the first woman to think she did not have what was already hers. The enemy came asking a question that she felt she had to answer. When she answered him, she backed herself into a corner. By responding to him, she fell into his trap and allowed herself to think she did not have what was already in her possession.

She allowed the enemy to convince her that she was missing three things: beauty, food, and wisdom. They were already around her. Eve was the first woman, and I am sure that God fashioned her with incredible care and great beauty. He then put her into a garden paradise, where beauty was all around her. Food was plentiful and available for the taking; there was only one tree she and Adam were to avoid. And wisdom? Eve walked with God in Eden, so she was face-to-face with the all-consuming wise One. Eve had everything she could possibly need, yet the serpent tricked her into believing she did not. Eve then fell into a pattern of thinking that the beauty, provision, and wisdom all around her were not enough. Isn't it just like the enemy to play such games? How often have I thought I had nothing to offer when God was busy clearing the path so I could finally see what He had put inside me? This happens to us over and over again. Although we have the beauty, wisdom, and provision of God at our disposal because of the sacrifice Jesus made for us on the cross, God is constantly working overtime in our lives, trying to redirect the same lie that consumed Eve in the garden.

THE POWER OF CHOICE

If Adam and Eve were given a "do over" in the garden, I doubt anything in our world would change. Even if Eve had found the strength to resist the serpent that day, the enemy would have tried to deceive her on another. The problem was not in the fact that Eve was given the power to choose. The ability to choose between yes and no, good and evil is a gift given to all of us at birth. Choice is not a bad thing. God gave us this gift because He wants us to choose to obey Him. There is something powerful in

9

doing so. God's greater glory is revealed when we choose to honor Him with our obedience.

It may seem as though life would have been easier if mankind could not mess up. But we know God does everything for a reason. So why did He give us free will? Without choice we would be automatons, loving God out of obligation instead of delight. This is not the kind of relationship the Father wanted.

For all the knowledge she lacked, Genesis Eve was educated in how to live out the reason for her being, which was relationship. Her purpose was to love God and reflect His goodness by loving Adam. Even after the fall, by doing this, deep joy and completeness would spring up and overcome her shallow flesh and bring security to her needy soul. Eve is usually remembered for her most famous mistake, but she is much more than one bad decision. And so are we. Even in her sin Eve is educating us so we can be wiser, better women of valor.

In studying God's Word, I have come to realize just how important choice is to God. In the beginning He gave us free will, and throughout Scripture we see Him reaffirming that freedom to choose. Our lives are made up of the choices we make each minute of every day. No relationship is formed outside of choice. You don't get up or go to bed without it. It is in every part of your life's cycle and knit into your DNA. Choice is the reason you turned toward God or away from Him.

If choice were not an option, what would your life have looked like? It is clear that God wanted us to have choices.

In the beginning of the Adam and Eve story God, after crafting and creating the world, inserted choice by way of a tree in the center of the Garden of Eden. He asked only one thing: that Adam and Eve choose not to partake of it (Gen. 2:16). But the instruction was never about a fruit. It was always about the obedience Adam and Eve would demonstrate in resisting the fruit.

God used His voice to bring creation into existence. His voice brought into being things that were never there before; then out of those things He designed and fashioned mankind. He formed man from dust and used His very breath to give him life. Then He pulled out a rib to make a counterpart for Adam. God did this with a great understanding of loneliness and a desire that man not feel its sting. After taking such care in creating us, God, motivated by love and a desire to bless, allowed us to choose whether to receive His goodness, which is why this gift of choice can be disastrous.

I have sat staring at Genesis 2:9 and wondering why God even mentioned that tree in the first place. Why let them know it even existed? Everything was perfect; why ruin it? In six days God extended His most creative hand. He spun planets, space, gravity, landscapes, and bodies of water; He created life of all kinds and ended by molding dust into humanity. Then, with all the splendor of creation to behold, He asks that one tree be avoided. Why not just take the tree out of the garden or keep it under lock and key? God could have done anything He wanted, and He chose to not only place that tree in the center of the garden but also to warn mankind against eating of it.

After inquiring of God about this, a profound thought occurred to me: choice must have existed before Creation. Scripture doesn't say much about the fall of Lucifer beyond what is recorded in Ezekiel 28 and Isaiah 14. Because of this, we really don't know what went down. What we can infer is that if Lucifer got puffed up enough to choose to rebel against God, free will had to have been in operation at that time. So the ability to choose existed long before God created Adam and Eve.

I'm not a theologian, but I am able to put two and two together and draw a conclusion. If Lucifer could lead a third of the angels in rebelling against God, then in the realm of the angelic and the supernatural a choice existed to believe or not to believe. Somehow a standard was set, and God's desire to be obeyed was made known. The same desire for our obedience was stitched into humanity. We were not created without the ability to obey; we were given the opportunity to decide whether we would. Our actions would then determine the direction we would take and the one we would serve.

Choice is important in our understanding of God and His relationship with humanity because when we make choices, they are usually provoked by a desire or need, intent or determination. God has always longed to be our choice. When we choose Him, He can reach us even faster with His transforming love, because we've stopped running from Him and are possibly even running toward Him. The day I chose Him changed everything for me. The spiritual DNA of God within me was ignited, allowing God to step in and show me all the things He wanted me to know, because I had chosen Him to lead me. Choice, yes, is key. Satan made a choice and fell away from God, taking many angels with him. This reveals another fact: choice brings with it the power of persuasion. People watch the choices we make, and they can be swayed to follow our example. Because choice existed in the beginning, the power for Satan to persuade Adam and Eve to follow his example also existed.

We must remember that when God was creating the universe (as we understand it), He already had an enemy in this fallen angelic being called Satan. As God was making the creatures, sky, and sea, His fallen enemy was spying on Him and devising a plan to thwart His purposes. Satan must have been aware of God's business. I mean, he was allowed to slither around Eden, right?

Many things are happening in the Genesis account that for years I failed to recognize. I have only recently seen the story within the bigger story. God had an enemy before He created mankind. That enemy sinned against God. So Adam and Eve were created in an atmosphere that already knew sin in the form of Satan's betrayal.

When He was creating the earth, God constructed a fruit-bearing tree to symbolize choice. If eaten from, this tree would bring an understanding of the darkness God's enemy chose. It seems that seeking to be like God—to rule and reign over our own lives instead of surrendering to

Him, to pursue honor for ourselves instead of giving God glory—is still what gets so many of us into trouble.

The Battle Is the Lord's

Now we must take a second look at all the scriptures that proclaim the battle belongs to the Lord (1 Sam. 17:47; 2 Chron. 20:17). Remember, God had an enemy before He made mankind. The fight against sin was raging long before we came on the scene, and it was God's battle to win, not ours. We make it our fight when we choose to disobey. In commanding Adam and Eve not to eat of the forbidden tree, God was asking that they choose not to become aware of the sinful rebellion that resided in the heart of his enemy before they were created.

After the fall of Lucifer, God established a place called Eden and within those gates created something new when He breathed into dust. God made man with the hope that what He created would give praise back to the Father rather than seeking to exalt himself. Mankind, of course, failed at this, but God must have known this would happen because He had a backup plan. I cannot imagine God making man without knowing that humanity would fall into sin and would ultimately need to be redeemed. The hope for mankind to obey is without a doubt in the heart of God, but the choice to actually walk in obedience is in the heart of man.

Eating of the forbidden tree was never about us being like God and knowing the things He knows. The Father knew that choosing to eat of it would lead to our understanding the rebellion lodged in Satan's heart and the potential for us to be persuaded to follow suit.

The enemy of God was looking for a chance to wound the heart of the Creator. In the Garden of Eden he found the opportunity of a lifetime. Lucifer, disguised as a serpent, goes after God's son and daughter—God's own hand-designed children, His great plan, His DNA. I wonder if this is why Satan sought out Eve first?

God commanded Adam not to eat of the tree in the center of the garden before He even created Eve (Gen. 2:16). God created Eve later out of a concern for Adam's loneliness and because she completed a picture of God's ultimate desire, which was to have a bride. Yet the enemy does not attempt to deceive Adam, who was first given the instruction about the tree. He goes after Eve. Why? I don't think this was because she was a girl and as such was "the weaker vessel," as many teachers have claimed. She at this point was Adam's equal partner. As part of her punishment for eating from the tree, God commanded her to submit to Adam as her husband. But before the fall, they ruled hand in hand.

God gave Adam and Eve the ability to do what He did—to create. Yet unlike Adam, Eve was given a womb in which to do this. This is important to see here in the education of Eve. Satan, spying, sees that Eve has been given the ability to produce a life. Who then would be the better one to deceive first, the one who gives the seed or the one who carries it?

I believe this is why Eve was sought out that day in the garden. By getting to Eve, Satan must have thought he would gain access to all of her offspring. What better way to exact revenge against God than to go after what He loves: His children, His chosen ones.

A woman's ability to carry life is no small thing. I see it as an incredibly beautiful gift from God. I believe the enemy could see that as well. This cannot be overlooked and disregarded in the process of understanding Eve.

I am in no way saying women were created only to bear life. But in our efforts to affirm the many facets of a woman, let us not lose sight of how wonderful and important that ability is. A woman's body was created to nurture new life. It is within her, in the "in secret" place Psalm 139 talks about, that God knits life together.

It is under a woman's heart that a small being is protected. It is her voice that soothes the child, and, sadly, it is she who can choose whether to end the life growing within her. How would we have another generation of kings and presidents, heroes and heroines if not for this important gift God gave women?

The enemy is cunning, and he would have thought about who to approach in the garden and how to do so. The devil's strategy was to plant doubt in the heart of mankind and let that doubt be passed down over and over again to future generations. Would that not be easier to do through Eve since she was given the ability to nurture the unborn? I think this is one of the main reasons the enemy chose to attack her first.

A PLACE FOR MERCY

Thankfully God always had a plan to bless and protect His children, and women were a key part of that plan. It is clear that God gave Eve a womb for a reason.

One of the Hebrew words translated "womb" is *racham*. I am no Hebrew scholar, but I know that many Hebrew words have a three-letter root system. Each of those root words houses deep meaning that can take your breath away. The word *racham* comes from root words that mean "to love," "to have compassion," and "to be compassionate."[1] Now consider that God gave Eve a *racham*, a place for mercy and compassion.

After Adam and Eve make the choice to sin and God pronounces their consequences, He addresses his enemy, Satan, by proclaiming that Eve and her offspring will be forever at odds with him. God declares, "And I will put enmity between you and the woman, and between your offspring and hers; he will crush your head, and you will strike his heel" (Gen. 3:15). It is in this verse that Eve hears of the day when a head-crushing Messiah will come from the *racham* of another young Eve.

In essence, God tells Satan that because he went to the woman to deceive mankind, out of her loins would come humanity's redemption. Hope eternal springs forth in the wake of one of the most devastating choices mankind ever made.

In the first moments a woman appears in Scripture, we are being educated. We are watching her movie play out.

We see her perfectly fashioned and formed character fail in a quick moment to hold on to truth, bending itself instead toward the doubt that a lie brings. In that one movement we see the unraveling of perfection. Yet we cannot see only Eve's flaws. Before we examine the consequences of her mistake, we must see in those passages the intention and the invention of something amazing and valuable.

The creation of a *racham*-housing woman has powerful spiritual and literal meaning. I believe that God, knowing all things, could not think about creating Eve without seeing how His Son would come into the world to redeem the creation He loves. After all, are His intentions not for His bride? I find it amazing that God would give women the ability to cradle life. This was not by chance; it was God's intentional design.

When God made you and me, He saw beyond our mistakes into the promise He placed within us—the hope for His kingdom purposes that He deposited within us at the start. Even our mistakes cannot erase the destiny God has placed on the inside of us.

You were made to carry life. Eve was the first to be handed that announcement, and she was within earshot to have heard God promise that mercy and compassion would come from her womb in the form of a Savior who would crush her enemy and bring life to humanity. God has placed the promise of victory within us modern-day Eves also. Within every woman is the ability to find compassion and mercy and to speak life over our souls.

As Eve's descendants we are in the middle of the same

fight to believe God's voice over the din of Satan's lies. How do we stop making the same mistake Eve did? Can we learn from her and stop doubting and questioning God? Eve walked out everything women will experience first, so she must hold some insight and revelation into the female journey. In our journey to find Eve, maybe—just maybe— we will learn from her how to see truth and recognize lies, to live with hope and demolish fear, to declare destiny and deny defeat.

I have been naïve for so long in so many ways. I have spent decades trying to win battles that were not mine to fight. Now I hear Eve shouting out to us to take a different route instead of falling over and over into the same pattern of pain by doubting our beauty, our worth, and our strength.

I have spent too much time pondering why Eve was never clever enough to ignore the serpent's voice. I wish I had spent more time seeking to understand the devil's overall plan in the Garden of Eden. The truth is, the devil was not after Eve or Adam; he was then, as he is now, after everyone who could choose to believe in Jesus as the truth and the way to find truth. How can Satan do this best? If he can derail our hope and get us to doubt the truth, he will get us to not only live in defeat but also to pass along the same doubt and hopelessness to the next generation.

This revelation can help us begin to live life the way we should. There is enmity between the enemy and us and our children. His name is Jesus. The enemy may come at us with an attack, but Jesus will conquer. No matter the devil's plans, God's victory is sure.

Something happened to Eve that day in the garden when her choice led to her dismissal. She was forced to wake up to the power of the flesh. She had lost the ability to judge correctly. The day she realized she wasn't wearing clothes was also the day Eve found out how mistakes can reveal your own nakedness. If she only knew then what we know now about the serpent's scheme, so much pain could have been avoided.

All of us have the ability to search out the matters of the heart. I searched out the matters of Eve to find why so many women cannot believe what God says about them. In finding Eve, I found the root to this insecurity. It begins for all women there in that garden. *"Did God really say?"* It's a question I'm learning more these days to answer with, "Yep, He did."

2
FINDING the GARDEN

It has been several days since we left Eden, and I am heartsick. We have been sent away from our home. I am trying to get used to our new surroundings. They are beautiful but not like Eden. I had no idea how special Eden was. Compared to where we are now, it was as if I was standing inside of destiny. The feelings I have now unsettle me daily. My sense of stability is gone. This I am most uncomfortable with. I asked God about this, and He said I feel guilt and shame that came with the choice I made. He said sin is what drove us out of Eden. This sin seems to follow us around and divide the air we breathe.

Adam is restless, and I hear him pray loudly to God for forgiveness. I cry a lot. I have poured out my heart to God.

I miss Eden. It was home. Now I long for the paradise God speaks of, where we will again be near Him.

We cannot return to Eden or to the time before the serpent deceived me. But we are told to carry on. Adam is to work the ground, and I must submit to him. That would have been easier to do in Eden. We think differently from each other now.

Adam speaks of revelation he has received for the soil. He talks with God about this. God is still our teacher. I still feel love abounding toward us, yet I often sit alone and ponder the state I find myself in. How could I have questioned my own Maker? Now I look ahead. As I learn about this place I am living in, I see choice on all sides. I question everything I see. My heart is always searching for what to do next and where to find rest.

I know too much, which feels strange since not knowing enough is what got me here. Now I just want to find peace again. I talk with God in this new place early in the day. Sometimes I say nothing and listen for His guidance and encouragement. The simple sound of His voice makes me remember what used to be. I long to stay there inside His voice.

TENDING THE GARDEN

A garden enclosed is my sister, my spouse; a spring shut up, a fountain sealed.

—SONG OF SOLOMON 4:12, DARBY

I'm not a professional gardener, but I like to think I am. I love going outside and planting vegetables and flowers in winter to see beautiful blossoms in the spring. For me, there is nothing more satisfying than walking into the house to the scent of my own hand-cut roses or smelling organic green tomatoes frying in the skillet on the stove. I have always loved a good garden. I think they carry rich symbolism. God put man in one at the beginning. A garden is where Jesus prayed to His Father, surrendering His will before He was to die on the cross. And in that same garden He was seized to stand trial and ultimately be crucified.

In His parables Jesus frequently mentioned seeds and planting, trees and flowers, often using them to symbolize our hearts. Just like soil, our hearts can be tilled so the seed of God's Word can be planted and grow. A bag of seeds can go a long way. What does that say about our hearts?

The name Eve means "living one." That is so appropriate, I think. She was pulled from the side of Adam, who was made from dust. She was the product of something God used the dust of the ground to create. In a sense, she was the first flower pulled from the garden of Adam's side, designed and purposed by a Maker who thought to number every hair on her head.

In finding Eve, I have had to find the garden of my heart, where I first felt loved and safe. I have always pictured my heart like the well-watered garden described in Isaiah 58:11. When I was sixteen, after I feel asleep at night I would meet God in a rose garden in my imagination. There I would hear His voice and talk through many things I needed advice on as I grew spiritually. Most importantly that garden is where I fell in love with God's ways and received revelation about His love for me.

I am a romantic and a dreamer, so it was not hard for me to conjure up a fictitious place in my head and meet God there. I would close my eyes and suddenly be there with God in that garden. It became my place to walk and talk with Him. Those visits became an important part of my spiritual development, and I often refer to those times in conversations with God. We had some incredible conversations in that garden. Over time as I became busier and busier, the more I longed for those unhurried times with God in that rose garden.

Our hearts are not literal gardens, of course, but I believe seeing them as such can create a powerful image. Think about your own heart. If it were a literal garden, what would it look like? Would it be well maintained, or would it need to be weeded because of worry, fear, anxiety, and daily pressures? Would it have good soil rich with faith, or would the ground be hard and unusable because of unbelief?

I often watch a television show called *Hoarders*. For some reason I find myself drawn in to these stories about people whose homes have become dens of unbelievable filth and waste. It is hard not to watch a reality show like this and not see all the chaos in the house as a picture of the chaos inside many people's hearts. Unresolved trauma, pain, fear, and grief can all cause people to hold on to things they should release. A heart, like a garden, must be tended. It will become overgrown and chaotic in the face of neglect. In a well-tended garden we find life, which is the fruit of the gardener's careful attention. No matter where you came from and the circumstances surrounding your birth, God's creative artistry is evident in every life. Whether you were born to a lost heroin addict or a healthy, loving parent, God is the One who formed you in your mother's womb and watched you grow. Every Eve is the handiwork of God. He took time to make you perfectly. Because of Him your life is beautiful.

As human beings we are conditioned to look at the natural before the supernatural. We are conditioned to look at what the flesh is doing rather than what God is doing to breathe life into our spirits. There is a reason God planted Adam and Eve in a garden. And there is a reason He will take us back to a paradise called heaven. The garden has much to teach us.

God took five days to create our physical surroundings. He spent the first two days making light and dark, day and night. He spent a day separating the sky and sea and calling land into being. Day three was about the plants and the gardens. It took Him one last day to gather some dust and breathe life into the man, and then a short time later He grabbed a rib and made man's counterpart.

God took His time with creation, and even now it sings of His love and splendor (Rom. 1:20). God's handiwork still bows, waves, chirps, splashes, roars, and worships Him without hesitation. Why is it that the one created thing He wants a relationship with questions, fails, falls, and struggles to believe there actually is a God?

I love Psalm 104. It describes creation's effortless ability to just be exactly what God told it to be. How often do we wander outside under the open sky and not realize what is actually happening? As we busy ourselves throughout the day, all around us God's faithful creation is worshipping Him. Our human ears cannot hear what God listens to constantly. Those trees in your front yard are shouting a thank-you to God that maybe you have forgotten to give Him.

God spent days making what would be our canopy of life and hope. God in all His wonder tells the sun to shine by day and the moon by night because He wants us to know His intent was to always keep a light on! Creation has a strength we do not. It is constant.

When man's sin became too great in the generations after Adam and Eve, God called His servant Noah to build a boat. The floods God promised came, and everyone was destroyed except Noah and his family. When the waters began to recede, the dove brought a branch from an olive tree as proof that the garden was growing again, that life emerged out of devastation. Hope bloomed like a flower in spring.

When I was young, my mother arrived home one day from her job as a church secretary with two branches from an oak tree she had been given out of our pastor's yard.

She had wrapped the ends in wet paper towels and sealed them in plastic Ziploc bags. Grabbing a shovel, she dug a hole in the lawn on each side of the small modular home we rented. Watching her from the front window, I laughed. I was certain that within a day we would see wilted dead branches flopped over on the ground. To my shock those branches took root and started growing into tall trees.

My mother was a faithful saint of a lady. She had a quiet, powerful love for God. She never sought attention and humbly served as the secretary of our small Baptist church for years after my father lost his life to cancer. My father had a deep passion for God too, but he was a bit of a zealot. This zealous nature had my mother trailing behind him on crazy adventures that were not always convenient but that my father was certain God had led him to pursue.

This made for a challenging time in their marriage and a season when my mother's trust had to be completely in God. We lived in absolute poverty because my father often lacked work, choosing to live by faith. There were six of us kids, and my parents never owned a home; many times we lived in campgrounds like wanderers.

My mother found solace in gardens. She loved plants and flowers. No matter how humble our home, she would dig a patch of dirt out back and plant corn and tomatoes. Into her garden she would escape to find a few minutes of peace and quiet. Often she would sit out there and read a used copy of *Sunset* magazine, envisioning the house and garden of her dreams. Sadly she never saw her dreams fulfilled here on earth.

In her small garden my mother would spend time in prayer—she was an amazing woman of prayer. When my father was diagnosed with cancer, my mother kept a vigil around his bed and faithfully prayed for his healing until the Lord took him home. Her intercession for my siblings and me, I am positive, is the reason we all made it through those difficult early years and still serve the Lord today. She was such a model of grace and trust in God. Her heart was rich with faith and her hope plentiful.

I remember stopping by that small, sad, old rental home fifteen years later. I was an adult and living in another state but back in town leading worship at a conference. I decided to take a trip down memory lane and drive by our old house. Now much more rundown, it seemed so tiny in comparison to the two massive oak trees towering over it. That home, where my mother took her last breath, still had her hope growing on each side of it.

I sat staring for a long time at those trees, tears running down my face as I watched those once small branches of hopeful possibilities now swaying powerfully in the summer breeze. My mother's faith in God seemed to echo in them that day.

Those trees were her garden in a time of great question and fear as she wondered how she would raise six children as a widow. I wondered if, as my mother watered those trees, she prayed that they would become a sign that she and her children would grow stronger and take deep root in God. Signs along the way are good for the soul.

HOPE IN THE RUINS

The LORD will guide you always; he will satisfy your needs in a sun-scorched land and will strengthen your frame. You will be like a well-watered garden.

—ISAIAH 58:11

A year ago I was asked to accompany my friend Maria Durso to minister in a women's prison in Baton Rouge, Louisiana. Maria and her husband, Michael, pastor Christ Tabernacle Church in Glendale, New York. Maria was asked to teach a small conference for the women in the prison, and she asked me to lead worship for her. I had never ministered inside a prison before and felt a bit intimidated, but I accepted Maria's invitation.

After we had been checked through security and retrieved our visitor name badges, we stepped onto the prison campus. I noticed the grounds right away. There were heavily secured fences rolled with barbed wire and flat-roofed brick buildings with concrete walkways in between. But in the middle of the grounds was something I would never have expected: rows and rows of impeccably manicured gardens.

There were rose beds and geraniums, hibiscus and Landis bushes along with many other types of green and blooming flower beds. The inmates bent over these gardens weeding, watering, and pulling dead leaves off stems for up to eight hours a day in the hot sunlight.

29

The irony of such beautiful gardens in such a place of wounded reality stunned me. I was expecting to walk in and see the harsh, gray slap of life behind bars. Instead my first picture of prison was the sight of a well-watered and -maintained garden. I was undone for days after that conference. I don't know if the faces of those precious women will ever leave me. Most of the women we met would live behind those barbed-wire fences for the rest of their lives. Yet in that place of despair, those Eves, young and old, were planting and preserving beautiful gardens.

It was a picture of Isaiah 51:3: "For the LORD shall comfort Zion: he will comfort all her waste places; and he will make her wilderness like Eden, and her desert like the garden of the LORD; joy and gladness shall be found therein, thanksgiving, and the voice of melody" (KJV). Even in a locked-down prison a garden could be found, a place of joy and gladness, thanksgiving and the voice of melody.

I spoke with many of the women after Maria preached. I did not need to ask them why they were there; they volunteered that information freely. They told me of how their lives had derailed and mourned the fact that they will never see their families again. One woman, whose face was disfigured by the severe beatings of her boyfriend, had been sentenced to eighteen years after her third check-fraud offense. She wept and kept telling us she was only trying to feed her children. I heard about murder, theft, drugs, and prostitution—women carrying all of these offenses in the midst of a lovely garden. I wondered how many tears had been shed as the women weeded the gardens in that prison.

Before we left we were asked to pray in the center of the compound. The chaplain told us that many illegal schemes are hatched and secrets told in that part of the yard. In the center of that compound, near the garden, the enemy seeks to still deceive and destroy those who are already bound.

Freedom can be costly, because sometimes giving up our will hurts more than giving up our bondage. But there is something about finding the garden of our hearts that brings us to a place of wanting to choose freedom whatever the cost.

Those inmates in Louisiana were in a place where the presence of God loves to be; I am convinced of this. Jesus did not come for those without need. He came for the desperate. He came for the Eves whom life has trampled on.

The stunning visual of a garden inside the prison did not hide the wounds or discredit the pain in that place. But it provided a picture of the hope that surrounds all of those prisoners. Even in their sin they still have the ability to maintain beauty.

There is not one Eve alive today who is not in need of hope. Everyone needs it.

When we find the garden, we find that hope. In every heart you can find good ground. And it is not so difficult to make something grow. In the natural you need good soil, some water, a bit of sunlight, and great faith. Spiritually, to make your dreams grow and hope spring forth, you need a willing heart, the redeeming blood of the Savior, and the light of the Son to reveal His plans for your life.

Dreams are very much like seeds. If you never plant them, you will never know if they will bloom.

How many Eves are not in an actual prison but live in a metaphorical one? I have met and ministered to so many women who don't believe God loves them enough to make them good at anything. I used to be much like them, but I have tasted the joy of freedom. I know the power of believing God's opinion of me. Experiencing freedom propels me to want more of it.

I am a visual thinker and a dreamer. I try to journal daily, and I love to talk God's ear off. In the middle of the garden where I used to meet God as a teenager, there was a gazebo. I would sit there with God and tell Him my deepest hopes and dreams.

During these times I heard Him speak some very specific and painfully truthful things to me. In that place He would speak hope and rest and prepare me for seasons of great pain and distress. I am grateful for that visual gate into God's presence. It has made me more aware of who God is and how much He loves us. I think this garden God allowed me to envision helped me realize how much He cares about me. Imagination can be an amazing tool God uses.

Gardens require patience. They require our time. If we leave them unattended, they either grow out of control or they wither and die. The same goes for our hearts. As believers, we should all be looking to grow more spiritually sound as we mature in our walks with Christ. It takes a conscious effort to weed out fear and faithlessness, worry and regret. Your "weeds" may be different from mine, but we both must be responsive to every area God shows us we need to become healthier in. We must be willing to look inside and weed any areas we have left unattended.

How do we tend the garden of our hearts? We must water with God's Word the dreams that have begun to wither. We must expose the enemy's lies to the light of truth. Unless there is water, there is no growth. Unless there is conviction and follow-through, weeds will choke out hope.

Eve was evicted from a perfect garden, but I believe she has found an eternal home in another paradise. God is a God of restoration. I often wonder if in heaven one day I will find the original Eve tending a beautiful garden. Of course, this time there will be no snakes!

3
FINDING OBEDIENCE

It is just dawn here. Adam and I have found a place to call our own. There is much to do. Since leaving Eden we have learned many things about surviving under this sun. God has spoken about shelter and shade. Food is found well enough, and I am learning to be clever in how I find it.

I am reaching toward His voice. Sometimes the emotions inside me are heightened. I still miss Eden. At night I dream about it. I dream about what that life was like and could have been if sin had not found me. I think of my life before remorse and shame stole perfect peace. Adam still blames me. It is where some of the restlessness in him comes from. It's a festering root. Love is evident, and God is near, but the resentment raises his voice at times. He works most of the daylight hours. I am amazed that he has the strength he does. *In many ways his body is so much stronger than mine. And the ideas Adam comes up with amaze me.*

I spend much time talking to God and learning how to be Eve without Eden. Obedience is what God seems to require more than anything. We provide offerings to Him, and we do this exactly as He says. God has become more specific. I desire to be trusted again. This is my hope at least. Every time we bring an offering I wonder if it is enough. I wonder if I should bring more to cover us for what I have done. God told me I must let go and receive His grace. He said grace draws us to obey, and obedience will point me toward peace. I feel this is truth. Now, if I can just do this well . . .

A HEART TO OBEY

> It is the LORD your God you must follow, and him you must revere. Keep his commands and obey him; serve him and hold fast to him.
> —DEUTERONOMY 13:4

When my son, Justice, was in kindergarten, one of the first Bible verses he memorized was "Children, obey your parents in the Lord: for this is right" (Eph. 6:1, KJV). I remember talking with him about what that verse meant. I am blessed to say that in the eight years of his young existence, he has been a very obedient child. I think this is partly due to his personality. But my constantly crying out to God to pour His truth into him hasn't hurt either!

I realized early on that Justice doesn't like to disappoint

me. There is plenty of free will in him for sure, but he has a God-given desire to obey. When he is disciplined, he needs to be assured that I forgive him. I have loved seeing this as a parent. God does too. I know He is right there with me as I lead Justice. I couldn't do this without Him. God is able to fill so many voids for single parents.

I was thirty-eight years old when I found myself still painfully single. During a trip to Romania I had an encounter with God, and He spoke to me powerfully about adoption. Six months later I became the mother of a tiny baby boy I named Justice. I knew even in my youth that I desired to adopt. However, the adoption did not happen the way I had imagined or hoped. It came after years of wailing and pounding on floors in complete anguish as I asked God where my husband was. It came after years of living with a kind of loneliness that seeks to kill all hope and extract any traces of joy from a person's life.

I was a young dreamer who had her life all planned out. I heard God's voice at a young age, and I was certain He told me I would marry and have children while I was still young. My life turned out much differently than I imagined, and it was nothing I would ever have asked for. But as I prioritized obedience over everything else, I found God's love for me deeper than I had ever thought possible.

I do not think I would have pushed to find this love if I had not experienced the fracture of pain and the pressure of loss. I spent many years asking why, but all the time I asked God why I never stopped pursuing His presence. My pain over not seeing the answers to my prayers may be what drove me to spend quality time with God, but whatever the reason, I got there. Experiencing God's tangible presence made me desire to obey Him more and more.

Every time I experienced the depth of God's love and devotion, there seemed to always be a cost in the natural. Yet the way it felt to hear and relate to God far surpassed the natural costs. The beautiful thing is that if I could do it all over, I would not change a thing. Through my trials I found a treasure: the power of obedience.

God put obedience at the center of relationship with Him. The fallout from Lucifer's disobedience in heaven and then Adam and Eve's sin in the garden are telltale signs that obedience is key to staying in right relationship with God. God does not require our obedience because He wants to see us squirm; He doesn't relish being the boss and watching us follow Him around as if we are slaves.

He made it very clear in the New Testament that He considers us friends, not servants (John 15:13–16). But obedience creates the proper balance in our interaction with God. It is what keeps our relationship with Him in alignment and keeps our lives in balance. It is the spiritual chiropractor we need to visit frequently and the glue that holds us together.

When something is not right or is out of balance in my life, the first thing I check is whether I have been obedient. Has God spoken something to me that I did not follow through on? Most of the time our baggage is the result of problems we created for ourselves through our disobedience. Many times we don't need to pray for deliverance; we simply need to obey.

If you run a stop sign, you might get into an accident. If you go over the speed limit, you might lose control of your vehicle. It's the same with obeying God. He put rules in place to protect us from all the things that could go wrong.

We are fooling ourselves when we think we can have a real relationship with God without obeying Him. God commanded Moses to tell the children of Israel how to reach the Promised Land. But because of their disobedience, they spent forty years wandering in circles in the wilderness. I wonder how many Israelites questioned whether God had given Moses directions in the first place. I wonder how many thought it was God's fault that they didn't know where they were going in life. Once a commandment is broken, it becomes easier and easier to deny it ever existed in the first place.

Obedience is a must if we want our relationships with God to flourish and desire to receive the revelation He offers. Obedience is for our own good. God guides us because of His great love for us. Sin will try to convince us that God requires certain things of us because He wants to punish or control us. Wisdom will counsel us to ignore that voice, surrender to God, and let Him lead us home. God sets boundaries because He loves us, and we obey Him because of our love for Him. There is no bondage in serving those we love. We obey what we love to serve.

Through the years in ministry I have seen a cycle in us as women. Our insecurities often lead us to disobey. Eve allowed unbelief to cause her to disobey God. Now we all have this in our family line. I have encountered hundreds of women who let insecurities about their appearance, their work, or their relationships cause them to disobey God's will. Then in time they find themselves crawling back to the throne room, wounded and bruised because they followed the trail of their insecurities into disobedience. I understand it. I've had seasons of my own when I obeyed my flesh in the moment instead of obeying God.

I think again about those women prisoners in Louisiana. Every day they are told what to do and how to do it. They don't get up or go to bed without being told when to. They live a life of forced obedience because of seasons of disobedience. Because of their rebellion against the law, they are now forced to follow rules without any kind of freedom at all. Disobedience woos us all the time. It whispers to us that we can have more freedom without rules, when in reality disobedience robs us of the freedom we have been given in Christ and locks us up for life.

A PROPHETIC PICTURE

After the fall God told Eve that her desire would be for her husband and he would rule over her (Gen. 3:16). Much later in Scripture husbands are told in Ephesians 5:25 to love their wives "as Christ loved the church." These two verses reveal a bigger picture that connects the Old Testament to the New.

God created humanity, and humanity sinned, but He

planned to send a Savior to free them from the power of sin. That Savior is described as a husband who will return for the body of believers called the bride. Could it be that God had Eve submit to Adam as a picture of what He would then ask of us as believers when Jesus comes as our Bridegroom? Is He establishing this relationship between Adam and Eve in Genesis because at the end of the story we are to be the bride who desires Him?

It is said that a wife needs to know she is loved and a husband needs to be respected. This truth can be confused when women don't respect their husbands as they submit to them and when husbands don't love their wives as Christ loves the church. When this happens, we become a mess of disobedient, resentful, untrusting companions. This is not the picture of marriage God intended.

A lot of people talk about submission as if it is a dirty word, and it is true that it has been misused and misunderstood at times. But I don't believe God was unloving when He made Eve reliant on someone else by having her submit to Adam. In the garden Satan intentionally went after Eve. The enemy didn't do this because he thought she would be too weak to resist him; he did this because he wanted to use Eve to reproduce doubt and unbelief in her offspring generation after generation.

In the punishment God hands down to Eve, we see Him establishing a covering for her, so the enemy would not have such easy access to the woman and the unique ability God had placed within her. Yes, Adam sinned too. But I believe that when God made the woman subject to him after the fall, He was calling Adam to "step up to the plate" and truly lead his wife and rebuke the enemy seeking to devour her and the children who would follow.

Through the years some in the church have used these verses about submission to allow what amounts to abuse within the home. In some cases the wife is given little or no say because the husband is "the head." We must realize that submission is not one-sided.

The name *Adam* means "dust" or "dirt." Notice that in disciplining Adam, God sentences him to work the soil. He becomes subject to the very thing he was created with. I wondered about this and spent hours in conversation with God seeking to understand the mystery in this punishment. I believe it comes back to submission. In order for the dirt to yield to Adam, he would have to work it into submission. In a similar way Adam would have to constantly resist sin and figuratively work his flesh into submission to God. In this we see the model of authority God established in marriage: Eve submits to Adam as he submits to God.

Although I believe wholeheartedly in this model for marriage, the truth is that all of us, married and unmarried, are to bow in submission to God, because He is the ultimate Groom and we, the church, are His bride. Both naturally and supernaturally I am to submit to Him. And if I am blessed to marry one day, I will also submit to my husband as a symbol of the Lord's divine design and of His desire to return for a bride who desires and submits to Him.

So many of us, male and female, struggle with submission. As a single woman I have had to be independent and strong, but being without a husband in the natural has only made me glad that we are required to submit to the Lord. Submission takes the pressure off me to have it all together, and it gives me a sense of security to know that God is watching out for me and steering me in the right direction.

Because I love God deeply, I submit to His authority as the Lord of my life. I know He has my best interest at heart and that He knows how to save the day. I have resolved that I am better off with Him than without Him. If I were ever to walk away from God, it would be because my flesh convinced my will to ignore the truth and disregard His wisdom. I realize that I need a leader to protect and guide me. I have no problem giving that respect over to God and one day submitting to a husband as the spiritual covering of our home.

Sometimes punishment is a blessing in disguise. God's heart for us as women is to lean not on our own understanding but on His wisdom.

In my earlier, limited knowledge of Eve, I held the opinion that she was to blame for the fall. In time I realized that I must rethink that idea. Was she disobedient first? Yes, she certainly was the first to partake of the forbidden fruit. She responded in weakness to the serpent, but so did Adam. We must consider again why the enemy launched an attack on Eve. He went after Eve for a reason—not because she was weak but because he wanted to manipulate her strength, which was to influence her seed.

Steadfast Through the Storm

Many modern-day Eves are facing seasons of shaking. My sister was recently in that place. She was married for twenty years and had five children with a man who was a wonderful father and seemed to love her. Looking back, she can see where their relationship began to fracture, but to most outsiders their breakup was a complete shock. As her sibling it was painful to witness the end of something that seemed so right. It was hard watching her fight to save her marriage and seeing the impact the divorce had on their children, ages three to eighteen.

My sister's heart was breaking, but instead of wallowing in despair, she ran to the feet of Jesus. She poured out her hurt to Him in a way that was both beautiful yet incredibly painful to see. God did not come down and patch her up overnight. He pulled her, stretched her, and waited with her when she was handed divorce papers and became a single mom. She had a million choices. She still does. But the choice I watched her make was powerful. She turned to God and trusted in His unfailing love.

There is something truly amazing in that. The Israelites wandered around in the desert for forty years because they allowed their complaints to derail their obedience. It is possible to obey God and still find yourself in a desert. But you will not enter into the land of promise—that place of rest—if you begin to walk in disobedience after encountering a trial.

I think of the biblical Eve and the road she walked after her departure from Eden. Where did she and Adam live? How did they communicate? Was their love deep and wide? Did they share moments of laughter?

Personally I think Eve was wise. I think she learned quickly after her encounter with the snake. I think she loved Adam deeply and was devoted to him. She was a gift to him. God made her for Adam because He understood the weight of loneliness. That is a profound thought, especially for anyone who has struggled with being alone. Eve was created to accompany Adam because God is aware that we were not meant to be alone.

This has encouraged me deeply. God is not OK with loneliness. It concerns Him. I have seen loneliness lead many into disobedience. Many leave purity way too soon and live with shame way too long because they didn't want to be alone.

I think of Eve as a girl like any of us, who struggled with the same issues we face. She had to deal with all the effects of the fall—feelings of insecurity, shame, fear, failure, and the like. Sin also affected her relationships with God and Adam, and the purpose she and Adam were created to fulfill. I am sure Eden was not the only place where sin knocked on her door. I just wonder if obedience didn't mean more to her when it did.

So many problems stem from a lack of obedience and diligence. If you are facing major hurdles, ask God to reveal any areas in your life that might not be in alignment with His will. If He shows you that something is out of balance, I urge you to choose obedience. It is the only way to get your life back on track.

I want my son to live a life of obedience. It is the main character trait I want to see in his life. I want Justice to long to obey God and the authorities He establishes in his life. But that begins with me. I must walk out obedience before Him, letting my choices light a way for him to follow.

4
FINDING PROMISE

It is night. The sky is dark, and the moon is hiding itself behind this beautiful, strong tree we sleep under. I have spent the day thinking about God's promises. There is a child growing in my belly, forming into a tiny version of one of us. I have no idea if it will be male like Adam or female like myself.

This is a season like no other. There is something overwhelming in what is happening. This child will be the first in creation—the first of generations that will stretch forth in front of us. I sit for hours alone with God, and we talk about this miracle.

As the weeks progress, this body of mine has become a wonder to me. The Creator has thought of everything. The magnificence of my design and what my gender can produce is beyond what this human flesh can contain. In this season I am aware of my flesh more than ever. The wonders of God never cease to amaze me.

I am drawn to that most. Thinking about His wonder and the authority He must possess to have given us so much takes my breath away. I still flinch when I think of what we have done in betraying Him. The pain of that is ever present, yet I feel an expectation for what we can become, and it calls me forward. I feel the Father's forgiveness, but I am never far from the knowledge of my failure. I may be most of aware of my desire not to fail; I feel it with every fiber of my being.

Everything Adam and I face is the outcome of what we have done. Even in this glorious time of expectation I remember the words of our Maker. I stare straight into His heart right now, weak and vulnerable, weepy and full of anticipation. I also fear. I fear what He said would be my punishment. He said I would experience pain. What does this mean? There has been so much discomfort since we left the garden, how will this compare? I am apprehensive. I cannot imagine the pain of delivering this child the way Yahweh has said I will.

I plead for grace and mercy, though I know I do not deserve it. Father speaks to me of promise. How does a God who has been betrayed by my own actions still speak to me about my life becoming a promise? Who is this ruler who has compassion on Adam and me even in our failures? I am becoming a mother as He has become Father to us. I cannot comprehend it all, but the spirit inside me shouts with a love *for God I cannot explain. I am to be a mother. I shall not be the last.*

My children will lead to promise. If my children lead to promise, then my life is full of promise. Our enemy the serpent will be at odds with my children and me. God said we would crush his head. How will this be? Do I have what it takes? Each day is filled with something new. I am full of promise and hope, promise and hope, promise and hope.

PROMISES KEPT

Promises are important to women. A woman will remember a promise when it is made. We like to be promised things— at least, I know I do. When a friend promises to come over or remembers my birthday, it means something. A promise is a deed of trust. It brings security in special ways to the hearts of women.

Eve was a reflection of God's promise. She was a reflection of His love, His talent, His deity, and His nature. And within her He placed the promise of victory over the enemy. Even after she sinned, God's discipline contained promise in the center of it. Eve would have to submit to Adam and experience pain in childbirth, yes. But she also would have someone to lean on in Adam, and when the pain of childbirth was over, she would have a baby to nurture and cherish. God is not a bad father. He can cut us and heal us all in one stroke (Hosea 6:1).

Eve was the first of us females to carry a child and feel pregnancy swell her belly. She felt the first flutter, the first kick. Think about her experiencing that with only Adam and God around to share it with. Adam was probably the first dad to be bewildered in the delivery room. How could he wrap his head around what was happening to his Eve? These are the kinds of questions that keep me searching for more of the deep things of God.

Over time I've come to realize that so much of the deep I'd been looking for is found in simply believing that God is a promise keeper. Let me explain what I mean.

One night while I was whining to God about His timing in fulfilling His promises, He gave me a revelation. I absolutely, 100 percent believe everything the Bible says. The stories, the miracles—everything! I began my Christian walk taking everything about the Word of God seriously. I bought into Christianity lock, stock, and barrel, and still today I would sell everything I own to defend the Scriptures. I believe Jesus was born of a virgin named Mary. I believe Jesus died in body and was raised in spirit out of a tomb. I believe He appeared after His death to His disciples and to others with whom He spoke.

I believe the Red Sea parted just as Moses said it did in the Book of Exodus. I believe blind eyes opened and the lame jumped up when Jesus touched them. I believe in some pretty crazy stuff I have read in that book—hands down, I believe it!

So why, then, have I had the hardest time believing God would answer my prayers when I'm in a struggle? As I was whining to God, I felt that question well up in my heart. I stress out about all it takes to raise a child on my own. I lay whimpering on the floor like a flailing fool, sometimes groaning out too many whys to count because it seems impossible that God would answer me. I can believe in a virgin birth, but I can't imagine that God would meet my needs. I was stunned and humbled by the revelation. Moments like these show us how solid our faith really is.

THE DESIRES OF YOUR HEART

Psalm 37:4 says, "Delight yourself in the LORD and he will give you the desires of your heart." It's easy to get excited about the "he will give you" part of that verse, but it's no accident that those words come after "delight yourself in the LORD." Scripture gently shows us here that within adoration there is a secret. God does not want glory just because He deserves it. I think it benefits us as well.

When we give away something valuable with unselfish hearts, something is released in our spirits. When we give our desire, which comes from God, back to God, it causes us to desire more of Him. We see a circle of love with one half completed when we understand that God loves us and the other half completed as we simply receive that love from Him. Receiving His love propels us to love Him back! God is the recipient as well as the giver.

There are many promises that I have yet to see come to pass, but I choose to delight myself in the Lord anyway. Although many of the promises I received from the Lord have not been fulfilled in the natural, I've seen more miracles and blessings than I ever dreamed I would.

Sometimes I wonder if our interpretation of what a promise fulfilled looks like is tainted. I've met many modern-day Eves who seem to feel more like redheaded stepchildren than daughters of a King. They've been waiting for promises to be fulfilled, and yet nothing has materialized. God created Eve knowing she would birth generations. From dust and hope in a rib came children of promise, rulers of kingdoms.

But when Eve rubbed her swollen belly for the first time in complete shock and amazement at what was happening to her body, was she thinking of lineage and inheritance? Was she pondering the bigger picture? In her body was the seed to a promise fulfilled, but could she see that?

She did not have our modern-day distractions, so I like to think she spent her time trying to walk better outside of Eden than she did inside of it. Maybe she spent time walking with the Lord, listening to Him, and trusting that He would keep His promises. But I'm sure that when she was holding her firstborn, she never would have imagined that he would one day become a killer. Would she have been able to trust the God who keeps His promises if she had?

To write anything about promise is a little difficult, especially if your promises have not come yet. I know how it feels to experience heart sickness waiting for God's timing to fulfill His word. I have learned (after many tears) that in those times of waiting, our focus should be on walking out a pure belief that in God is the fulfillment of all our promises. He is the reason our lives make any sense at all.

When I think about all the women who have had to endure trials like the ones I've gone through without God, it is arresting to my spirit. I don't know how I would have survived much of what I've gone through if I hadn't met the Lord when I was a child.

I have waited, and am waiting, for many of the promises God made to come to pass, but still I can boldly declare that God is a promise keeper. God promised a Messiah in the Old Testament through prophetic shadows and types. The prophet Isaiah declared, "For to us a child is born, to us a son is given, and the government will be on his shoulders" (Isa. 9:6). God fulfills this promise in the New Testament.

That promise wasn't wrapped in a big box tied with a bright red ribbon. Jesus was born in a humble manger, grew up in a carpenter's house, and ended up being beaten, spit on, stripped naked, and nailed to a cross. That Son of God rose from the grave shouting to our souls that we have an inheritance in His kingdom if we believe that He was the promise fulfilled. He is the promise and the fulfillment of the promise. So when I receive a promise in the natural but don't see it coming to pass, I have to choose to believe that God *has* fulfilled it in the Spirit.

"In his heart a man plans his course, but the LORD determines his steps" (Prov. 16:9). I have waited for years to see the promises of God fulfilled in my own life, to actually see the things I felt or heard spoken by the Lord come to pass. I realize I can plan my life even with the guidance of God, but it is ultimately the Lord who will direct how it goes. I am desperate for Him to lead as I follow. If I were being completely honest, the waiting part of life has not always gone well for my flesh. Our flesh does not understand the timing of the Lord.

There are some things—deep, deep things—that are in our hearts only because God birthed something in us to believe they could exist. It wasn't good for Adam to be alone; he needed Eve. As I have already mentioned, God knows what loneliness can do to the heart. I believe He desires marriage and companionship for humanity. Yet He has seen fit to have me walk out so many years of my life's journey as a single woman.

My experience has changed my view of what it means for God to fulfill His promises. My interpretation of favor and blessing has changed as well. How much favor does one need to be blessed? That depends on your idea of blessing. I mean, most of us think of blessing as something we receive. Although there is some truth in that thinking, God's favor and blessing are much more than the giving of material things. His blessings are not just things that can be seen by our naked eye. Some of the most profound blessings we can receive are experienced in our spirits.

I have journals that I have filled over the course of more than thirty years, and their pages are full of promises and words I have heard the Lord speak. Many of those promises have come to pass in various ways; others have not met their seasons. All of those journals, however, have become my scripts to God. Many circumstances in my life have left me baffled. I never thought I would be unmarried at the age of forty-five. I didn't see barrenness in my future either. I didn't expect God to allow the deaths of so many of my friends and family members.

I have had low times when I could have allowed the enemy to convince me that there were no promises left. But God continued to draw me to belief. When my mother was in her last weeks of life, my brother asked her why she thought God was allowing cancer to take her life. My mother looked straight into his eyes and proclaimed, "God did not come to save my body but my soul. He has my soul; I am at peace with my body's ache."

She had come to a place of surrender. She knew God's way was higher than hers. This world is full of sorrow. We will all walk through trials at some point in life. Those are times to learn so much more about God's power.

I don't understand much of what life has brought my way so far. I have attended and sung at so many weddings only to go home and cry myself to sleep because those weddings were not my own. I have believed and encouraged the dreams of others only to be betrayed by those I thought were friends. I have traveled to minister in cities around the world only to come home to an empty house. I have watched my peers' music rise to the top of the Christian music charts and had my own music declined by radio stations because they didn't like my sound.

I have been flabbergasted by what my friends earn from their music sales, knowing that I'd left many worship events wondering whether I would be able to make ends meet. Yet I have had a fire in my bones to believe that no matter what life throws my way, God still has something more for me. I was certain that God called me to minister through music; after spending so much time with God, praising and worshipping Him, I came to know His voice. So I kept the candle burning and a light on in the window of belief.

The passion I have for the Lord kept me desperate enough to hang on and see Him in everything, even in the pain. I know that joy comes in the morning. If God would not give us joy in the morning, He would not have put it in Scripture. He can be trusted.

SINGLE PEACE

I made a commitment to follow the Lord at the age of five. At age sixteen I asked the Lord to find my husband and to bring me only the man He had chosen for me. God seemed to hold me to that. I mean boy, has He ever! I once thought the husband I had prayed for had come, but the Lord made it clear that he was not the one.

I desired to be married at age twenty-six. I prayed fervently, yet my twenty-sixth birthday came and went, as did many others that were met with private weeping and questions to God about why my life had taken this course. I stopped clipping wedding dress pictures out of magazines by the age of thirty. Eventually I ended up throwing away the folder where I had kept them. I did get bitter. I became bitter and then sad. I stayed sad for a while and then became mad.

I yelled and pounded on the floor asking God why over and over. I questioned everything. My flesh was hurt by what I could not understand, yet I did not stop pursuing God and always let Him pursue me during that time. I still do not understand God's timing, but I knew then as much as I do now that I needed His love. So I surrendered. We have to.

We have to learn surrender in times like these, when God's timing causes our hearts to ache. If we do not, we end up drinking out of bitter waters. I have not yet seen in my personal life what I desired and deeply felt God said would come to pass. Yet I have seen God become the promise. I have felt His presence, and nothing compares to the peace of His presence. Personal desire fails to compare to the simple joy of His presence.

I said good-bye to another dream in February 2011. The nurse handed me a piece of paper when I was in pre-op. She told me to read over it carefully and showed me where to sign. She knew as well as I did how serious that document was. By signing it I was acknowledging that the operation I was about to undergo would render me "unable to conceive a child." I'd fought so many fibroid tumors that they finally ruined my uterus and threatened my life.

I lay on that stretcher in the hospital staring at the ceiling in disbelief. "That's it, huh, God? This is how it ends? All those years of hearing You say I would bear a child, and this is what You allow?" Silence. I could kind of feel my heart crack. Then I heard the Lord whisper a simple, "Rita, no matter what, I love you."

If this had been the five years before, I would have been a little more sarcastic and cold but not now. I had come to a fork in the road and asked God to drive. He'd been driving for a while when this occurred. So I simply said, "Jesus, You have my life, my love, and my devotion. I now willingly hand over my uterus." In that moment what I found was peace. In that moment I understood the words my mother had spoken to my brother when she lay dying. God had my soul, and I would have to entrust my body to His hands as well. There was still grieving and deep sadness, but what lingered longer was peace.

The revelation of why He had asked me to adopt six years before hit me in a sobering moment. He knew! He knew that six years later I would be in a medical crisis, so He started healing me of my hysterectomy six years before I even had it.

What about the promise He'd given that I would have children *plural*? Those children are, perhaps, the students I mentor in loving God and making sounds in song. I mean, do I really know the mind of God? He had promised me something but gave me so much that I never expected. Is it enough? How many more children will I adopt or mentor? Maybe piles and piles.

And there will be promises that will seem to have been unanswered, and I will never know why on this earth. But my goal is no longer to see the promise fulfilled, but to know the One who is Himself the fulfillment of promise.

There may be moments when just pondering the word *promise* makes your insides thrash around and your feet tap nervously on the floor. You may pivot in your chair and sigh heavily. That word *promise* looms over a broken heart like a bad day repeating itself. Yet in order for us to believe and love a God big enough to stitch us together in our mother's wombs, we must also believe in promise.

We must also believe that the way He orders and directs and moves and provides can be known in us only if we have allowed Him full control. "*Full* control?" you may ask. Yes! God is a promise keeper! I mean, why would He make a promise He has no intention of keeping?

We can know God and even be known by God, but we can never think that His ways are like ours or that He will do exactly what we *just know* He's going to do. I meet people everywhere I go who received promises from God. I mean, these folks have big God stories, where the promise came exactly the way He told them it would. There are some really cool accounts in Scripture of God speaking something and then doing it exactly the way people expected. But in all the cool stuff God does, He asks for faith and trust before He does anything.

God has asked us to live by faith, and if we do so, we will see fulfillment of the promise. God made a huge promise to Abraham and Moses, and they saw great things come to pass but at great cost. Abraham became the father of many nations, but he waited twenty-five years for God to fulfill His promise. Moses led the children of Israel out of Egypt but not before persecution of the Jewish people intensified. Will we carry the promise if it comes at a cost? God gave a word in Psalm 37:4–6 for us to obey: "Delight yourself in the LORD, and he will give you the desires of your heart." In our obedience to follow and respond to Him, we will see the promise of God fulfilled in our lives. No matter how you slice it and serve it up on a spiritual platter, sometimes all the waiting can get personal. For women, it can get real personal. I roll my eyes a bit when I see young women in their teens and early twenties frantic over not finding a date or a husband yet. I have handed them tissues as they wept while sitting with me on my couch or at a coffee shop. They described feeling bitter toward God for making them wait all of two days for a man to come into the picture. I chuckle on the inside when I hear them complain because I know this is hardly a hardship. Although I would not wish for other women to endure, as I have, such a long season of singleness, when I pray with them, secretly I ask God to give them eyes to see the husband Jesus before they get distracted by Mr. Right. Timing is everything.

A PROMISE IS A PROMISE IS A PROMISE

I am no longer twenty-six, and I am still not married. Outside of a miracle, I will never conceive a child, one of many dreams I still hope for but have not yet seen. But I love God more now than ever. My perspective has broadened, and I have grown in wisdom because my eyes are set on Him. I am consumed by His love. I am no longer bitter. I am still able to keep oil in my lamp and praise the Lord.

You see, a promise is a promise is a promise. I would not

be who I am in God if it were not for His promise over my life.

Why does the cost for me sometimes seem higher than the cost for others? That is a mystery to me. Maybe it has to do with something God wants to pour out of me when I worship Him, or perhaps it relates to what I must carry as part of walking out my calling. I can't think of one disciple in Scripture who didn't have a rough journey in life, because speaking truth came with a price. Why would I be any different?

We were all made to worship something. If creation never ceases, then that is a clue that the desire of God's heart is to be worshipped. This isn't about God being self-centered; it's about so much more. I have found this really amazing place where as I worship God, giving Him the glory in and through every emotion, I move closer to things promised. I believe that hidden in the adoration of the Lord is a secret supernatural gift that we can receive.

When we choose to worship, the Spirit of God restores our souls and moves us forward in relationship with Him. We gain peace with God. The only way to find this place is to walk into it. And the only way to walk into it is to praise God through the sorrow and be willing to risk believing in things yet unseen. There is blessing in the simple fact that you are breathing, alive, healthy, and able.

Finding promise is finding Him—the fulfiller of everything we could ever ask for or think of. When God is found, He pours promises into us and pulls away the façade or the people we hide behind. In Him there is no mistake, and when we decide to live in Him, we must cast away the thought that we were mistakes. He pours hope into us and dries the tears flowing down our cheeks. Remember, all of Scripture is a promise that He would defeat sin at a cross. He fulfilled that promise with His coming. Will you promise to follow Him?

5
FINDING TRUST

I am a hollow creature. I am full of life, and yet it is this fullness that causes me to realize how full of Yahweh I need to become.

The Maker says our minds have the ability to wander, and lately I find myself wandering both in thought and in body. God speaks phrases and paragraphs that are full of mystery. He tells us that Adam and I are central to something—it is beyond our ability to comprehend. With the weight of this mystery bearing down on me, I find myself wandering about, wearing paths as I circle and circle in conversations with God.

The words He speaks have such impact that I stop to build small altars of remembrance to Him with stones. Now there are altars scattered all around. I ask questions, He speaks revelation, and I build reminders. I do not want to forget. Yahweh says the nature of sin is to make us forget His grace. Yet God's nature is to remind us of the gift that we do not deserve. These stones are small collections of reminders I have built for myself.

I am aware of my sinfulness. I am so unlike Yahweh. I do not compare to His perfection. Sometimes I think I should not come too close, but He beckons me forward. Something great is coming, and I will be the first to hold it up to Him. I think this soon-coming child will create a new way. Father says it is simply a new path to journey down.

This journey makes me aware of my own fearful state. I am losing memory of the me who knew the safe haven of Eden. The me that exists now, the one who was persuaded to fall, has lived longer than the one created without sin. Day returns like night returns, and we mature in our human state. Human. I feel humanity taking the lead and spirit gasping for air.

I feel the kicking and the turning of this life inside me—handmade, creative mercy knit by a loving Father and ever-forgiving God. Who am I? I am Eve, yet I wonder who I am at daybreak and then again at sundown. Who I was before I shared my body with another—first with Adam, then with this child—is unclear to me now. I am about to become a mother, and I am trembling at the thought. Adam looks at me, and I see questions in his eyes. So much is unknown despite what Yahweh tells us. He experiences the

*waiting with me, and together we circle and call to Yahweh
for answers.*

*Our Maker speaks again, telling us how He shared
Himself when He made us, and one day His body will also
be shared in saving us. I find more stones to build altars.
I must remember that conversation.*

Lost Trust

When I was in my twenties, I worked for a wealthy family
as a private administrator. I loved the job because I found
great joy in serving and in organizing things. One afternoon during tax season I decided to take a break and
asked my boss's accountant to go for a walk with me. My
boss lived in a very beautiful area with a private road that
wrapped around a lake. While on our walk, this precious
coworker began to share with me a frightening experience
she'd had while in college. She recounted being attacked at
knifepoint by a man who broke into her college dorm at
night. I remember being quite horrified as she told me how
she barely escaped with her life.

I asked if this incident was the reason she wasn't a
believer in God. She looked at me and chuckled, then
explained that the attack that night was the reason she
believed there *must* be a God. It was clear that she was
not in relationship with God, yet she was sure He existed
because she had survived that attack.

I wondered what I would do if I something like that had
happened to me. Would I be able to continue loving God

deeply? I probably would have faced an incredible emotional struggle. I could not imagine surviving an ordeal such as this woman experienced, yet it was this encounter that solidified her belief in God. Others have experienced similar things. I think of the Holocaust and war survivors who testify that God walked with them through the horrors they witnessed. How were they able to see light in the darkness?

So many women live fragile lives. When the pain we experience shatters our trust, we tend to put self-preservation at the forefront as we rebuild our lives. I am constantly surprised by how many women I meet who have little to no trust left in people, let alone God.

Faith and trust are two different gifts that we must grab hold of. Faith is confidence in God; trust is a commitment to remain sure of His love for us no matter what circumstances may come. These two are different, but I have found that they thrive off each other. When my trust in God is steadfast, my faith soars. If my faith is high—if my confidence in God's goodness is secure—my trust tank is full, and I know that nothing can separate me from His love (Rom. 8:35–39). But when there is not much trust, faith's pulse wanes and can even fail (Luke 22:32; Heb. 10:35).

If we commit ourselves to trust God, we can become like a mountain that cannot be moved (Ps. 125:1). We gain confidence in what we believe, which makes us more stable in many areas of life. Once trust is shattered, though, we become lost and need help navigating back to a place where we can take the risk to trust again.

Psalm 71:20 says, "Though you have made me see troubles, many and bitter, you will restore my life again; from the depths of the earth you will again bring me up." There is nothing so broken that God cannot rebuild and restore. When I ponder Eve's plight after the fall and the new life experiences she would encounter every day, it is not hard to see that she would have had to learn to trust and walk by faith. Imagine: you have been fashioned out of a bone from your mate, and you awake one day to see the one who made you and the one for whom you were made.

You were created with understanding of most everything and given freedom to make choices. You are told that you will procreate. Out of your body you will deliver a small version of your kind, made in the image of the one who created you. As if that weren't enough, you realize that you are the only one who can do this.

Then after your first big step out into this new place, you blow it based on the knowledge you have. The deceptive words you hear make you question whether what you have is good at all. You think it's possible to be like your Creator. Then you find out that you were terribly wrong.

So now you are living after the fall, trying to grasp how to retain what you have learned and teach it to your offspring. All the while you are experiencing what has never been felt before—the process of carrying another human being—and you will be a model for all who follow. I don't know about you, but I think that's some pressure.

With all the pressure Eve faced, what is most important is that in those precious beginnings she had God gently loving, teaching, and guiding her through every turn and broken road of her journey. How do I know this? Where do we see this in Scripture? It is not there word for word. But I know this because I know how God is with us. Has His love for us changed? Has He created us inferior to Eve? Are we less marvelous in His eyes than was she?

I am certain there isn't an emotion we as women have felt that Eve did not experience first. The scenery looks different and some of the foods have changed, but the emotions and strain that life on earth brings is the same. When sin put a wedge between us and God, trusting Him became a treasure. It is now up to us to redeem our idea of Eve and stop defining her by her failure by letting God redeem us in our failures. We must allow God to heal us and soak us in His redeeming blood. If we do this, we become the essence of what He designed us to be. We begin to emanate trust and faith, and we radiate the goodness of God's unconditional love for all to see.

LUMPS UNDER THE RUG

I take careful notice of the trials that come my way. None of us can escape the difficulties of life on this earth, but have you ever stopped to consider what kind of trial you are attacked with most? When I find myself struggling with something, the issue at hand is typically the polar opposite of my gifting. My main gifts are encouragement and worship. So what I find myself struggling with most often is discouragement and isolation. The enemy may be sneaky, but he's not original. He uses the same strategy over and over. Becoming aware of the tactics the enemy uses against you can help you avoid getting caught in his net.

I had a dream years ago that I was in a church setting, and the carpet on the floor looked like it was in need of being restretched. In the dream the voice of God told me to go to the corner of the room and begin to pull the carpet back from the wall. As I did this, I realized that what appeared to be lumps in the carpet were actually women lying under the carpet of the church! Still in my dream state, I presumed to know why these women were there: bad male leadership, religious spirits, etc. I was surprised to hear the Lord say that most of the women had rolled themselves under there by choice!

That was some reality check. I started wondering how many of us hide away, blaming everything and everyone for why we cannot move into our destiny, when the real culprit is our own insecurity and self-focus.

I understand strongholds and generational curses. I believe in deliverance and prayer. But what has helped to liberate me the most is realizing that no matter how bad I have had it in the past, only I can allow what was to linger and distort what could be!

What I long to see more of in the body of Christ is women who will take up an Isaiah 52:2 standard and "shake off [their] dust" and believe in the truth that God has given us the ability to free ourselves from the chains around our necks. We can read about this and preach it over our own souls, but until we actually do it, until we actually shake off the chains, we will live in bondage.

For some women who have to weed through years of abuse and suffering, discarding their chains can take time. There some are levels of shattered trust that take years to heal and rebuild. The beauty is that God is great at rebuilding everything. I have heard stories at altars that were so severe I had to later ask God how anyone could survive such trauma! But I know God can nurture the spirit back to a wholeness that we could not imagine.

The sweetest part of ministry through the years has been the letters and e-mails I receive, full of testimonies from women who were at their lowest points of darkness and trusted God enough to let the light in. All He needs is our willingness to trust and obey. When we stay willing, little by little God will reignite our hope. We serve a God whose goodness is more incredible than the shame we may have felt.

We need to become women who trust God with our lives instead of entrusting our lives to gods. We do this daily when we give ourselves over to the gods of image, anger, resentment, or fear. Roll yourself out from under that carpet and lay down the insecurities that got you hiding there. The issues that caused you to hide may have come through no fault of your own, but you must be determined not to stay in that place.

How do we find ourselves in these places? I have heard many women say, "I don't know how I got to this place of depression or darkness." When we find ourselves so far away from where we started out in our faith, it is hard to remember all the choices we made that led us to that place of regret. Regret and reluctance have so many women dropping down to roll themselves under a carpet like the one in my dream. It is not always the fault of the church or leadership or men. In fact, that is a point God seemed to be making to me in that dream. For some women it is abusive authority figures and church pain that cause them to bury themselves and hide from ministry. But for so many others it is a personal choice to give up and stop believing.

Have you ever been there? I have. It is not a comfortable place to be. I remember well contemplating whether believing God was worth the agony I faced. I have felt depression lower itself close enough to wrap around my mind and start a fight with all the truth I had known and believed. There have been days when I wanted to drop to my knees and roll myself under the weight of another excuse. I remember wanting to disappear and succumb to the lie that God would not come through.

Just as I know how it feels to despair, I know what it is like to not just listen to truth but also to arise in strength and draw it from my side like the sword that it is. Sometimes the only way you find your true strength is to rise up and take a stand. In Mark 5:41 Jesus takes the hand of a child who was presumed dead. Jesus says to her, "*Talitha koum!*" (which means, "Little girl, I say to you, get up [or arise]").

God is doing this on a daily basis for women who have

presumed themselves dead in spirit and in truth. He is finding them in houses and hallways and churches and pulpits. They are in grocery stores and sitting next to us at soccer games. They are women who are not living but surviving without light. God is speaking *"Talitha koum"* into their spirits and encouraging them not to see themselves as a lost cause. This too is my desire, and it runs deep. I want to see these women arise and behold their chains falling from around their necks. I know this is possible through the power of trust and belief.

Every woman's story is different. I have heard so many stories that have left me speechless. I also understand why it can take so long to break free of the past. When the road is littered with agony, it is harder to see where it actually can lead. Scripture promises us hope. That hope is sometimes all we need to begin taking the risk to trust again.

6
FINDING HOPE

My swollen belly tightened as the dawn arrived. What I experienced is unforgettable—the first of something greater than I can express. The agony in my flesh I will never forget, but the pain handed me a small, wailing trophy of perfection. I was speechless, and for long periods I just stared at his face, tracing his features with my fingers. We named him Cain.

Seeing him for the first time outside the womb that Abba in His wonder had created was like nothing I had ever experienced. It still feels fresh, new, and I find myself singing. I sing in moments that I used to spend contemplating how to get through the mess we made in the garden. I look down at this young, innocent collision of Adam, myself, and God, and feel honor and hope. Who is

73

he? Will he grow to look just like Adam? Will he act like his spiritual Father, Abba?

I remember the intense pressure I felt many sunrises ago when my Cain pushed his way out of the cradle of my flesh and into the field where I lay. I was drained and fearful when he finally arrived. I remember calling for Adam, my voice a pitch I had never heard come out of me. Fearful, I wondered if Abba was done with me. Was this what He meant by pain in childbirth? The words of God resounding in the garden pierce me again, reminding me of my decision to betray Him. This was my punishment, right? He spoke of birth and the timing of that birth. Was this it?

What had been an uncomfortable tossing and turning for months had me bending over in agony with every crashing wave of pain. Adam, helpless and wide-eyed, called out to Abba for direction and help. He encouraged me to stay alert and conscious of the signals my body was giving. I had been stunned that my body could have swollen like this anyway. How would it survive the rendering of this infant? I was in amazement that even though these contractions felt like death they were actually part of the process of producing life. Who is this God we serve? He who is grand in His design of us now hands us such responsibility to honor the new life He has designed within.

In some moments, drenched with sweat and exhaustion, I wailed for Abba to be merciful and render me done. There were hours of stabbing pain followed by moments of relief. I wanted the garden more than ever in those moments. Before Cain emerged, I wanted Eden back, and I pled and begged God for the release because all I knew in the moment was that I was falling and He was not catching me.

Cain came and with him sudden relief. I was in shock, and Adam was on his knees staring at the screeching babe on the ground. I heard Adam sobbing and singing God's praise. Then he let his head fall back and wailed toward heaven. The sounds of Adam crying and Cain screeching rang out like a symphony for God. Adam carefully picked up Cain and lifted him high over his head, tears still streaming down his face. "Abba, Abba," he cried, "You alone have done this. You alone are God." He repeated those words over and over, then his voice suddenly became quiet. He handed Cain down to me, and we were silent for some time, in awe of the Father and broken by His goodness to us.

The baby is quiet as he sucks his own hand. The three of us remain quiet in the presence of Abba God. Though soaked with sweat and blood, and weary from strain and pain, I feel relief and life and hope. I am in awe of God. In His mercy He brought me the joy of becoming a mother.

I am the mother of Cain.

A Tree of Life

Hope can be a hard habit to maintain. The Bible tells us that faith is the "substance of things hoped for" (Heb. 11:1, NKJV), but "hope that is seen is not hope" (Rom. 8:24). Who hopes for what she already has? It's like on Christmas or our birthdays. We may hope to receive a certain gift, but once we open the package there is no more reason to hope. The box either does or does not contain the desired item. I like to say that if faith is the evidence of things unseen, then hope must be the engine it runs on. Hope keeps our faith alive as we look forward to things that have not manifested yet.

Many women struggle with hope deferred. Proverbs 13:12 says, "Hope deferred makes the heart sick, but a longing fulfilled is a tree of life." It is easy to understand what it means to be heartsick, but what does the tree of life look like? I have experienced great heartsickness as I have waited on God. I continued to pursue God in those seasons because I longed to discover that tree of life. In my seeking, I have come to understand the tree of life, and I've found that though the tree is different for each of us, it always has the same elements at its core.

Somewhere in the healing of heartsickness God gives us the grace to see life in whatever He brings. He allows us to realize that He fulfills our longings—it may just be in ways we weren't expecting. We win the battle over hopelessness when we learn to become satisfied with the life that God brings, no matter what His timing is and even if it doesn't look exactly the way we thought it would.

A pregnant woman is a great prophetic picture of the conception of hope and the birthing of a dream. Isaiah even uses a pregnant woman to describe Israel's struggles for liberty (Isa. 26:17). I have met many women who have shared stories about their pregnancies, and a similar thread runs through them all. Some had easy labors and some long and hard ones. Some were bed-ridden because of complications while others say the nine months flew by without a hitch.

Some babies are born perfectly healthy while others fight to survive. The family with the healthy child can give glory to God for such a gift, and the family of the unhealthy or miscarried child has the choice to the same. The fulfillment of hope is not just about the end result; it is also about the heart's posture through the journey.

Outside of a miracle I will never conceive a child because of a health complication. What about the fulfillment of my longing to be a mother? My son, Justice, who was carried in the womb of another, became my longing fulfilled. I could have lived life filled with regret because I never gave birth to a child myself. If I had done so, I would have missed the powerful tree of life God brought me in the form of adoption. When I embraced that gift, the enemy lost his ability to steal my hope.

This is not as cut-and-dried as it may sound. Between the heartsickness and the tree of life are days, months, even years of surrendering to God the desires of our flesh and laying down our need to explain or understand our circumstances. Not releasing our need to have our longings fulfilled *in our way* creates a storm that will toss our belief all around. Even in the agony of what feels like defeat, God can pave a way to a longing fulfilled. Our perspective sometimes has to change in order for us to be led there.

There is a tree of life for those whose hope has been deferred, but there may be a cost to obtain it. We all have desires, and for some that desire runs deep. Have you ever known a deep desire that does not cause you concern or make you impatient as you wait for it?

Life is a journey we walk out. It will take living twelve months to complete a year. We cannot hit a rewind button and return to a month that has passed. We must wait for that month to come again with the passage of time. In much the same way there is a process to the plan of life and a process to receiving the promise.

We live within a fallen world, and maintaining faith and hope can be a tough road. That's not to mention the challenge of trying to maintain hope while carrying a promise around in the pocket of your heart! There is always a process to receiving the promise, and there will always be an outcome, though it may be different from what you were expecting.

HOPE DEFERRED AND HOPE FULFILLED

Eve must have asked some huge questions during her first pregnancy. I cannot imagine what it was like for her to give birth to Cain. She had no doctors or nurses, no pain medications or midwives. Perhaps worst of all, she may not have had any idea what to expect since no one had ever experienced birth before. All Eve had was a patch of hard ground under the sun or stars, and Adam, most likely staring blankly and fumbling around asking God what to do.

With only God to direct her and Adam to encourage her, she gave birth without being educated on how to have a baby, hold a baby, or nurse a baby. Eve was an original— the first woman ever to discover "what to expect when you're expecting."

In that first birth there was hope. Remember, the pain she experienced in childbirth was recompense for her dis-obedience in the garden. So feeling those pains had to remind her of God's initial punishment. I doubt she was able to feel them without thinking of what she had set in place through her sin. She was the first to feel this kind of pain, but even though she didn't have medical help, she had a just and righteous God attending to her.

At that point she would have had hope in God to push her through the pain. Hope in that moment was all she had to hold on to—hope that what was coming was a new reality that could possibly bring greater revelations.

During the months of pregnancy Eve knew she was with child, of course, but she had no frame of reference for what to expect outside the instructions she may have received from God. Just think about that. Can you imagine enduring labor or delivery without any knowledge of what to expect? Would not that first birth be exceptional?

I have saved every tooth that fell out of my son's tiny mouth. If I care about the memory of a first tooth or its loss, how much more amazing would it have been for Adam and Eve to experience the first birth? It is front-page news when babies are born at the stroke of midnight on January 1. How much more important, then, would this first birth be?

But this first birth was not the only significant one. Does not every new birth reflect a new season? Even the prophets in Scripture use a woman giving birth to declare a change of seasons. I figure for this first new mother, birthing that baby brought with it a ball of emotion. Every mother wants to believe having a baby is a sign. This new mother Eve would have been no different.

Hope is what my friend Kim had when she was told she could not carry a baby but got pregnant anyway. God has used Kim's journey to teach me about hope deferred and hope fulfilled. I have known Kim for years now. She and her husband desired to have children. But Kim's doctors warned her that getting pregnant would not be easy due to complications from the severe endometriosis she suffered from for years. Kim and her husband, Pat, believed God for a miracle, and though their journey was long, Kim eventually conceived and gave birth to two beautiful daughters. After witnessing such a miracle, Kim believed God had said He would bless her with a third child. So with the same hope she had for her previous pregnancies, she believed God would bless her to conceive a third child. She had two girls; now she wanted a boy. But her body declined to oblige. Her uterus was impacted due to endometrial issues, which caused many other problems. She was even hospitalized for other related issues and had to undergo multiple surgeries. At one point a doctor told her she had a "rotten uterus." In other words, there was not much physical and medical hope for this new dream to be fulfilled.

I watched my friend struggle to hold on to hope for several years as she received difficult diagnoses, and even endured the losses of her parents and younger sister. We had long conversations about heartsickness and why God seemed so far away at times. Yet I watched her always come back to faith and trust. Kim was desperate to find the tree of life.

Kim stood beside my own hospital bed encouraging me with hope and making me laugh in pre-op before I lost my own uterus. I understood Kim, and she has understood me. I did not tell Kim until much later that before the hospital staff wheeled me off into surgery, I had said a prayer. I asked God to give Kim her baby boy, to heal her own uterus and fill it with hope. I knew she would have and hold her son one day.

It was almost a year later when Kim called to say she had seen another doctor and was advised to have a hysterectomy to clear the mess that her body was making. She and her husband had prayed and came to the conclusion that they should surrender their dream of conceiving a third child. Maybe they would adopt.

The date for Kim's surgery was set. She and Pat had peace about their decision. But a week before her surgery was to take place she found out that she was pregnant! We were all beside ourselves with shock and joy. We were amazed by God's goodness. Hope lit up in our community of friends and family who were privy to Kim and Pat's journey. Best of all, it seemed the baby was completely healthy.

I ministered with Kim two months later in a meeting where she was asked to tell hundreds of ladies her testimony. It was amazing to see her courage and joy. Kim was expectant and beaming. I watched her call barren women forward and pray for them. Weeks after that service church staff sent word that many of those Kim prayed for had become pregnant! Kim was a living testimony of the Lord's faithfulness.

Less than a month later she went in for a regular checkup, and during the ultrasound the baby's heartbeat began to fail. Kim was rushed to a specialist who gave her the grave news that no heartbeat could be found.

When I heard the news, my stomach turned. Surely God was not going to allow this! Kim and her husband prayed for a miracle, but the baby's heartbeat did not return. She had to be induced and delivered the following day. I couldn't begin to imagine how that must have felt. She gave birth to a tiny baby boy, her child of promise whose very existence had filled so many with hope in the brief time he lived. Pat and Kim named him Samuel.

We are all still seeking understanding, and we believe that one day revelation will come. I have never lost a child, so I cannot fully relate to what Kim experienced. But we all can relate to the pain that follows the dashing of hope upon the rocks of circumstance.

During that tough time Kim's husband, Pat, wrote a note to friends thanking them for their prayers. He then quoted Hannah's declaration in 1 Samuel about God hearing her prayer for a son. Pat stated that he and Kim had asked God for a son, and God gave them the desire of their heart. Of course, the story didn't end the way they thought it would, but Pat boldly thanked God for answering them all the same.

As I read the letter, I was undone. I could feel hope rising up in the midst of grief so deep. It prompted me to sit with the Lord and talk through my own struggle with Samuel's passing. It just didn't make sense. Does pain like that ever? I turned to 1 Samuel 1 and read the story of Hannah over and over. I was very familiar with the account, but when I read it this time, I was listening to hear God speak into my sadness for Kim.

The Cry of Hannah

First Samuel 1 tells the story of Elkanah and his wife Hannah. Hannah was barren and desperately wanted a child. Her rival, Peninnah, Elkanah's other wife, already had children, and she ridiculed Hannah for being barren. Hannah's desire to have a child of her own was great—so great, in fact, that she prayed so fervently at the temple that Eli the priest thought she was drunk. Her lips were moving, but she'd prayed and cried for so long no sound was coming out.

Imagine praying so hard and so fervently that your pastor accuses you of being a drunkard! When Eli confronted her, Hannah explained her desperate desire to have a child. Eli answered her, "Go in peace, and may the God of Israel grant you what you have asked of him" (v. 17).

Hannah was desperate to be heard by God. There is a deep need in all of us to be heard—to actually know God is listening to our cries. I believe that Hannah's desire for a child wasn't as deep as her desire to have God hear her. This is where faith steps in; it is what enables us to trust that God will hear us and respond. Our flesh is constantly tempted to doubt. Faith is what keeps us from wavering.

Hannah had hope, but she also needed a response. After her visit to the temple, that response finally came. Stunned by Hannah's persistence, Eli the priest prophesied to her that indeed a child would come. The Bible is not clear on how long the waiting period was, but it seems to me that she may have received her answer sooner than later. Hannah conceived and bore a son, whom she named Samuel. She then did something extraordinary. She weaned the child and then took him back to the temple and left him there to be raised by Eli, just as she told God she would.

As a mother it is hard for me to imagine this. All Hannah

wants is to be a mother. So she goes to God and begs Him to give her this desire of her heart. God blesses her with a son, and she turns around and offers him back to the Lord—not simply in a special service at church but by actually leaving him to be raised at the temple without her. This act is stunning to me, and it points to a powerful truth. Being heard by God can mean more than receiving what we ask for. When God responds to our prayers, it emboldens our hope, causing us to keep engaging with Him.

First Samuel 2 begins with Hannah's prayer to God. Here Hannah begins to boast in the Lord and speak of His power. There is something breathtaking in this passage. In 1 Samuel 2:5 Hannah says, "She who was barren has borne seven children, but she who has had many sons pines away" It would appear that Hannah might be comparing herself to a barren woman who has had seven sons. Why seven sons? Anyone during that time who'd had that many sons was considered blessed. Hannah had given birth to only one son, whom she had just dedicated back to God.

There is a cross reference for this portion of Scripture found in 1 Samuel 1:8. In this verse Elkanah is trying to console Hannah in her grief over being unable to conceive, and he asks her, "Hannah, why are you weeping? Why don't you eat? Why are you downhearted? Don't I mean more to you than ten sons?"

Hannah was the one Elkanah loved. It was to her he gave a double portion. He was distraught by her anguish. Some of us might see him as selfish here, wanting his wife to be OK so their lives could return to normal. But I believe his words are prophetic.

I believe Elkanah is a symbol of the Lord in many ways; he is much like the Husband God who calls the church His bride. In our anguish and desperation to see results, He wants us to know that He longs to be better to us than the answer we are seeking. He wants to be desired ten times more than what we are asking Him for. We cry out for the pregnancies and the husbands to come. We anguish in prayer over the job or the healing that we need. Sometimes those deep needs can mean more to us than the satisfaction of knowing God. Can our prayers get in the way of God's answer? Only when that very prayer becomes an idol. Did Hannah have a revelation of this? Hannah pressed into God for results. She had a problem, and she needed an answer.

In her anguish her husband asks her a question about his importance to her, because it seems to be of less value to her than the answered prayer she seeks. After this talk Hannah went to the temple and told God that if He answers her prayer she will dedicate the child back to Him. Eli the priest then comes in and accuses her of being drunk. She explains her situation and receives an encouraging word from the priest.

In that moment there is a switch. First Samuel 1:18 says that after Eli spoke that word over her, she asked for favor and then got up. And when she did, her "face was no longer downcast." So what happened? Why the peace all of sudden?

Something transitioned for Hannah. It is interesting that her husband, who was also a priest, asks her about her love for him and then Eli declares over her the peace of God. The peace came when she left her request at the feet of God and surrendered to His results—*His* results, not hers.

Many of us are challenged to contend in prayer for what we are crying out to God for. Contending is good. It's scriptural. But we need to know when to lay our burden at God's feet and embrace the peace of knowing that God has heard us rather than holding out for certain results. Hannah transitioned to peace the moment she surrendered to God's results. She knew she had been heard, and peace flowed. However God answered was up to Him.

When God does answer her prayer, Hannah keeps her promise to give the child back to Him. I am not sure how I could have left my young child at the doorstep of a temple for Eli to raise—not after all the tears I shed to get him. Maybe this is love revealed and hope rising.

Hannah's reference to seven sons in her prayer is found again in Scripture, this time in the Book of Ruth. Naomi had been living in a foreign land with her husband and two sons because of a famine in Judah. She lost her husband and both her sons, and was left alone with two daughters-in-law. One daughter-in-law, Orpah, decided to return to her own people. The other, Ruth, promised to stay with Naomi and return with her to Judah.

Naomi is humbled by Ruth's commitment to her and sets out to find Ruth a husband in Boaz. She doesn't merely want to see Ruth happily remarried; she also wants to see her well provided for. In Ruth 4 Ruth has married Boaz and has given birth to her son Obed (v. 13). As they celebrate the birth of this child, Naomi's women-friends sing over her, "He will renew your life and sustain you in your old age. For your daughter-in-law, who loves you and who is better to you than seven sons, has given him birth" (v. 15).

Now it's a daughter who is worth more than seven sons. Naomi lost so much and tasted bitterness all along the way, but she believed that God would redeem not only Ruth's life but her own as well. And after all she endured—after leaving her people and returning in a destitute state—Naomi ends up part of the lineage of David and ultimately Christ by way of her grandson, Obed. Who would have thought that after losing her husband and sons Naomi would end up in the line of kings?

I think of Kim and Pat again and the loss of their precious Samuel. I am struck by the thought—overwhelmed really—that God must sometimes allow us to lose what we cherish in order for His purposes to be fulfilled. Sometimes it is after losing our Samuels that we find our Davids.

Without the loss of her sons, Naomi would never have had a grandson in the lineage of kings. I don't know how the Lord will reveal His purposes in my friends' lives, but I have watched them respond as Hannah did and give their own Samuel back to God, trusting His will over their own.

They too have found peace in their surrender. But I

know God is a God of restoration, and I am confident that He is going to heal Kim's heart after such a heavy loss.

Eve was the first to labor in prayer for change and courage. She was the first to hope for her child and the first to be disappointed. She would have had to hold on to hope for every promise that followed her out of the garden. Hope, no matter what.

Answers do not always come easily. Sometimes they come through years of prayer and petition. Breakthrough happens when those prayers become not idols but rather moments of surrender that take us deeper into the heart of God. Even when we have to give up our Samuels, we must still find a way to worship. The beautiful answers we seek come when we are in His presence. There He is able to show us that in our losses there is gain. Sometimes just knowing that God hears us means everything.

Life's snags may attempt to unravel our hope. But if we will surrender our way for God's, we will find the tree of life.

7
FINDING INFLUENCE

It is not quite dawn yet. I am awake with Cain, who loves the night and will sleep with the sun. I pray with fervency in this stillness before the sun makes an appearance. As Cain feeds and makes little noises I have grown to love, I close my eyes and feel grateful. Cain has already changed so much; he fascinates Adam and me daily. He has given us a deeper reverence for Yahweh and His power to create. Everything is small about Cain until he is hungry. The cry of hunger that comes out of this small being can send animals scurrying away! This makes me laugh because it's as if all of Adam's strength is embodied right there in Cain's hunger howl.

New emotions surround me. I am more aware of innocence and obedience, my flesh and its betrayal. There is great desire within me to preserve Cain and keep his way pure. I feel fear and an urgency to protect this baby who needs me in so many ways. If I do not feed Cain, he will not survive. If I do not console him, he will not quiet. When I hold him up to my face, he looks into my eyes and smiles as if I am all he loves and needs. I want to always need God that much.

Yahweh can see through to my heart. Cain is teaching me how to lean on God in His sovereignty. This also must be the plan of Yahweh to rescue us and bring us back to a "before" of some sort.

I must teach Cain the ways of Yahweh. I find myself having dreams for Cain and asking Yahweh what his life will be like and how he will honor God. I am aware that I can direct this babe to love and obey the Creator. I long for more little ones who will grow to be living, breathing continuations of the goodness of God. My spirit feels as if everything I am walking out is a word God is speaking. And every word He is speaking I am learning as a language to release back to Him in worship.

He is good, and He is great. I am stunned by how He thinks I deserve to love one so small like this. He trusts me with this love that stirs in me for this tiny son. I want deeply to teach this new, fresh somebody how not to stumble out in life but to stand with assurance and awareness.

I must listen. This birthing of Cain made me realize that I am so weak, and God is so strong. It is here that God hands me a living responsibility that is great even though this child is so small. I sense my inability emerge, my fear of failure rise, yet I somehow feel prepared for this *task. How can love like this wrap itself around a heart so quickly? Is this what Yahweh feels for us? His mercy dances over His judgment. His mercy is as stunning as the sunrise.*

Cain's name means spear. Maybe God will use him as a tool to sharpen our knowledge. He said that Cain was given for His purpose and because of His great love. I think everything Yahweh says or does is perfection in a way I cannot fully understand. I am fearful to ask Him of future things. In Eden I became aware of my flesh and frailty, my fear and failure. I do not want to fail my Cain. I want to hold him forever.

Yahweh says Cain will leave us one day and cling to his counterpart. I don't care to think of this now. Right now a wife is useless to him. I am what he needs. I shelter Cain against me and hum songs to him that Yahweh overhears. I sway back and forth and finally Cain slumbers. Cain sleeps and I stare at the rising dawn. Dreams are coming, and I will hold fast to their shouts of hope. What do dreams carry if not hope? And what does hope carry if not a chance to dream once again?

A Special Gift

All women have been given the gift of influence. Wherever life takes us we have the opportunity to influence others, to lift the chins of those around us, whether in the home, the workplace, ministry, or among our circle of friends. I call this influence a gift because it is more than a mere skill; it is part of our makeup, something deposited into us by the One who knit us together. Sadly we women do not always recognize the influence we were given. If we did, we would spend more time influencing those around us and less time being under the influence of things other than the Spirit of God.

So many of the dreams we have for the future are built on the belief that we can influence others. We want to do great things for God's kingdom, to see Him break strongholds over our families or nation, to see our spouses and children healthy and prosperous, to advance into more senior positions in our careers. We dream of making an impact, whether on the whole world or within a particular sphere. But so often those dreams fade over time as life happens, and with those lost dreams goes the hope that we can influence the world around us.

I spent many years thinking I would dream less over time, but the opposite has happened. I allow myself to dream more now that I am getting older than I ever did in my younger years. As I have grown in my relationship with Christ, I have understood more fully that without a vision I will certainly perish. So to keep vision alive in my heart, I started asking God for more impossible dreams. It takes faith to pray for big dreams because big dreams usually involve big risk.

I do not dream just because I want to see things happen; I dream to feel alive. Whether what I long for actually becomes a reality in my life is not my primary concern. I am encouraged simply by having dreams and aspirations because they bring hope and life to my spirit.

Women have a great capacity to dream and create, yet so often that potential is left untapped. I think of the dream I mentioned in chapter 5 about the women under the carpet of the church. So many dreams are perishing within us. One lie attacking our worth, ability, creativity, or the like can cause us to crumble. And our enemy knows when that happens all our dreaming will collapse along with us. He's always looking for one good hit.

We read in Scripture that we are to have vision and remain full of hope for the future, even as we age. Joel 2:28 prophetically declares that when God's Spirit is poured out on all flesh, sons and daughters will prophesy and elderly men will dream dreams. One purpose for that verse is to give us hope for the future, because it shows that in the future God still plans to do amazing things. He will accomplish those amazing things through people who remain alive to dream and press in to God no matter how life stalls their new seasons. This is why the enemy loves to get us to stop dreaming.

God's dreams for us are big. Many women do not realize that they were born to influence others. Becoming free of my own common, daily encumbrances opened my eyes to see how much influence I have. I am often caught off guard by the way the normal routines of life hem me in. Minutes, hours, and days can become more about accomplishing the tasks at hand than about how those tasks can possibly encourage my influence. Smiling at the grocery store checkout clerk and calling her by name can give her a whole new outlook on her day. If only we could slow down long enough to think of sharing our influence in such moments.

It is human nature to become consumed with our needs or wants rather than to live a life of influence. It is a choice to throw life and hope on others. We all carry this ability. Women carry it in some especially beautiful ways.

Isaiah 42:10 tells us to "sing to the LORD a *new song*" (emphasis added). This verse is powerful. The phrase "new song" is written only nine times in Scripture. It means we are to sing to the Lord a fresh new sound. With these words God is asking His people to forget the former thing and prepare for what is to come. Having the sense that something new and fresh is coming from the Lord sets us up to encourage others to expect more.

I don't have influence just as a worship leader or song-writer. Those gifts can influence people around me to worship and be creative, yes, but they are only able to do that because of the well those gifts are drawn from. All of us need to discover the fountain that our potential influence springs from and the power source it's connected to. Water always comes from a source. What is the source of our influence? Who or what is influencing us?

Do others want to be around you? Does your tongue speak life or does it speak death? My mother used to always say, "Garbage in, garbage out." I don't know about you, but I tend to steer clear of people who have more negative feedback than positive. I long to be around people who make me feel like I can conquer the world! Our lives intersect with others on a daily basis, and we are all potential encouragers to a dying and lost world.

I have been painting a picture of Eve as a reference for us as women to not only see her as real but also to see her as a reality check for the legacy we leave in life. In case you didn't think what you leave behind matters, it does! I am not talking about material things you leave to your loved ones; I am talking about spiritual traits you share throughout your life.

When I mentor people in worship, I am not trying to get them to act like me, sing like me, or write like me. I want to influence them to follow God first, and I encourage them to believe that He created them to do specific and incredible things with the gifts and abilities they have been given. I want to influence them to be all God created them to be, not to be like me.

When I became a mother, I was made more aware of this ability to influence. In my search for Eve I realized influence was knit into me to give away, especially to the next generation. When Justice was born, I became so much more aware of the things I had not been willing to give up for God. I didn't even recognize these things as sin until God highlighted them to me when I brought Justice home. I obeyed and started laying those things down because I didn't want Justice to carry around negative habits later in his life.

Some of that surrendering was painful, because what God brought to my attention wasn't just about daily tasks, personality glitches, or TV shows or movies that were inappropriate to watch with a child in the house. God also challenged me to evaluate which friendships and ministry relationships were healthy and which ones I needed to release.

When Justice's innocence came home, that mother's instinct was awakened in me and brought with it an awareness of areas of procrastination that I needed to address. It even became apparent why God had spoken to me to name my son Justice. A sonogram had indicated that the baby I was adopting was a girl, so I had chosen the name Liberty for "her." I had sensed the Lord saying a freedom was coming into my spirit through this adoption, so I figured it would be appropriate to call this little "girl" Liberty.

Needless to say I stood stunned and lost for words as I watched Justice's young hero of a birth mother push not a girl but a baby boy into the world! It was then that the Lord spoke to me out of Isaiah 42:3: "A bruised reed he will not break, and a smoldering wick he will not snuff out. In faithfulness he will bring forth justice."

I knew then that Justice is what God had promised when He spoke of bringing freedom. When this little miracle shouted out his first cry, everything as I knew it changed. *I* changed. I knew that by becoming his mother, I was also stepping up to the plate to protect his life from anything in mine that would hinder his faith. From the smallest to the tallest issue, I asked the Lord to show me what to let out the door of my life. I didn't want anything in my life that would disturb Justice's chance of living life well.

When Justice was born, I had a new sense of the kind of influence I would have in his life. I realize that not everyone feels this, but I did. I love God so much that I want to represent Him well to the next generation. I will not do this perfectly, but I will try hard at it.

How many things will we not accomplish as women because we refuse to dream or believe we even have a right to dream? How many opportunities will we pass up because we do not grab hold of the fact that we are women of influence? It is hard to believe we can have such influence if we are raised to believe we are worthless. I am tired of meeting women who seem to feel they have to apologize for allowing their words to take up air space. God fashioned us to find strength in His empowerment and confidence in His ability. If we women were conceived in the mind of God, don't you think He has a plan for us? We are more than we choose to believe we are so much of the time.

Mothers have the ability to raise sons to be kings and daughters to be queens. When I became a mother, I started dreaming not only for me but also for my son. My prayers for him began to reflect the dreams I had for his future. I don't know what he will decide to do with his life. And though I hear the Lord telling me wonderful things about his gifts, I would like to influence Justice to pursue God with all his heart and get his own revelation of his gifts and calling. My desire is to give him all he needs to make those great decisions for his future. This does not mean I don't share with him what I think God is telling me about his abilities. It just means I influence Justice toward enhancing his strengths and leave room for him to dream his own dreams.

I also benefited from being older when I became a parent. I was able to watch other people raise their children and gain insight into how not to impose my dreams on my child. My dreams can turn out to be just that—*my* dreams! God knows exactly what I need to raise Justice. He is the best parent out there!

I have dreams for Justice, and I want to use more of my influence as a woman of God to teach him how to follow where God is leading him. I am aware that as I gain more emotional and spiritual freedom in my own life, I will be able to pray more effectively for my son and make it easier for him to follow me to the feet of Jesus.

The more I desire to see God impart Himself into every aspect of my life, the less debris I will leave on the trail for my boy to trip on. Much of what children suffer from is the effect of unresolved issues that the generation before them left scattered on the battlefield. I am so desperate to live in freedom and have an open sail on the ship I'm navigating through the waters of life.

MOTHERS AND SONS

While seeking God about the contents of this book, I came upon some really beautiful revelations that I had never seen before. Keep in mind that before I began writing this book, I had a negative and limited view of Eve's character based on what little is said of her in Scripture. One point that was brought to my attention was the fact that Eve gave birth first to a male child. I felt God wanted me to see this fact in particular, and I believe it speaks to something that is pretty amazing.

We know God created man first, even though He always had the intent to create woman. And Scripture tells us Eve gave birth first to a son. Because I am naturally inquisitive, I asked the Lord if there was a specific reason that Eve's firstborn was a son. Why does God take such care to highlight this fact in Scripture? Could it be, perhaps, that God wanted us to see how careful He was to show Eve that though she was made subject to a man, she would be the first to shape a man into the kind of person a woman would need him to be?

It's from a woman that a man gets his first impression of love, compassion, and guidance. In his *Survey of French Kings*, author Walter Baxendale wrote that "of sixty-nine monarchs who have worn the French crown...only three have loved the people, and all those three were reared by their mothers without the intervention of [other teachers]."[1]

Mothers have great influence on their children, both male and female, but I want to focus on the unique relationship between mothers and sons for a while here. This is not to exclude single women or women who have only daughters. In the next chapter I will talk about mothers and daughters. I write as a single mother who adopted a son, but what I am sharing does not apply only to women who have natural sons; it is just as relevant to women who are spiritual mothers of sons. We must understand that some of the way we as women have been wired is due to the instrumental role our gender has been designed to play within the lives of others.

It's true that a father can teach his son how to love a woman through the example he sets in the way he loves his wife. However, many men first learn what it means to love through their relationship with their mothers. There is truth in the saying "behind every good man is a good woman." A good mother will raise her son to have strong character and become a great king.

When I applied for adoption, the agency I used said that they would be OK with me adopting a girl as a single woman but not a boy. It was not their policy to even allow single people to adopt, but they were willing to make an exception for me with that one caveat. They believed a boy needs a father, and I understood that. In fact, I was relieved that they wanted me to only adopt a girl, because the thought of raising a boy as a single woman was frightening to me.

The woman who chose my profile as a prospective adoptive parent had told me that an earlier sonogram confirmed she was having a girl. I had a closet full of pink and purple clothes, so needless to say I had to scramble to quickly figure out how to care not for a daughter, but a son.

God had obviously hidden the sex of the baby from both the agency and me. He had destined me to raise a son! I sense that God allowed the events to transpire just the way they did to strengthen me in knowing that God has a very specific plan in His heart for Justice. Knowing this has caused me to press in for even greater understanding of how to raise the opposite sex without an earthly father in a way worthy of my call as a mother and Justice's call to be a godly man one day.

Now, of course, I cannot imagine ever not having a boy. But there are times when I feel sorry for Justice. He's had to shop for perfume with me, and he learned pretty early on how to take out the trash and load a dishwasher and a washing machine. I've taught him how to clean up and the differences between what boys and girls like. My goal? To make him an amazing man of God and a great husband someday. His wife will thank me.

When a man grows up, he leaves his parents' household in a different way than a woman does. The Bible says in Genesis 2:24–25, "Therefore a man shall leave his father and his mother and hold fast to his wife, and they shall become one flesh. And the man and his wife were both naked and were not ashamed" (esv). I love that in this beginning for both Adam and Eve God reveals His plan for marriage.

I find it interesting that so much of what we find in the Word simply points us back to the Lord and illuminates who He is. In small statements God reveals a bigger picture. His own Son's future would one day reflect the words in Genesis 2. Not only in the natural would a man leave his parents to cleave to his wife; Jesus would do the very same thing spiritually.

When our children are babies, we dream about their futures, but a mother knows she will have to release her boys one day so they can cleave to their wives. The bond between mother and daughter may change over time, but they can remain very close. Yet a mother must release her son to develop a unique, God-ordained bond with his wife. This instruction for a son to leave and cleave is more than just God's plan for marriage; it is actually prophetic. Let me explain.

God does not design anything without a purpose. Eve was fashioned out of Adam's side, and her name means "living." God foresaw the role women would play in world history and the church. He saw the influence we would have as mothers that would affect lives for decades and even centuries. He was also aware of the insecurities we would struggle with and that we would long to have our value recognized.

God knew that many women would struggle to view mothering (in any capacity) as a great gift. So He placed within us a deep value for love and gave us all we would need to teach a man how to love from infancy. We were perfectly designed and incredibly well thought out to the last detail.

What happens when a man lacks a mother's loving influence? I have seen TV interviews with male prison inmates who say their mothers never loved them, and they claim that is the reason they got involved in crime. Without guidance and the sense that their lives mattered to someone, they became self-destructive.

God makes us aware in Genesis 2 that a man will have to leave his father and mother and then cling to his wife. When a man marries, he is warned that he has to detach from what was and attach himself to his new wife. God raises that banner of instruction over the first couple in the garden. Yet it foreshadows something that came in the Old Testament and was then lived out in the New.

I found another verse while studying Scripture that led me to this precious insight. It is in John 19. Jesus is hanging on the cross, dying for the sins of the world. His mother witnessed Him being nailed to the cross and is now watching helplessly as He suffers. The disciple John is near her, and when Jesus looks down and sees them, He speaks.

> When Jesus saw his mother there, and the disciple whom he loved standing nearby, he said to his mother, "Dear woman, here is your son," and to the disciple, "Here is your mother." From that time on, this disciple took her into his home.
>
> —John 19:26–27

I cannot imagine the heartbreak Mary must have felt in those moments when her son hung on the cross, this Mary whom God had on His mind when He created Eve with a womb so that His Son could take residence in one someday. The all-knowing God saw young Mary in the eyes of a young Eve. He knew the journeys both women would take with their sons, and He knew they would share in similar heartbreak. From Eve to Mary these mothers of sons would have to let them go one day.

This exchange in John 19 was Mary's last encounter with her son. She had felt every contraction, was there for every baby kiss and hug. And now she had seen Him beaten and humiliated, spit on, and crucified. Jesus speaks little while hanging on the cross. He addresses the lost man near Him, who was also being crucified. He speaks to John His disciple, He speaks to His heavenly Father, and He speaks to His mother.

It is what Jesus says to Mary that has captured my heart. Under all the weight Jesus is carrying while hanging on that cross, He looks down to see the woman who carried Him, loved Him, fed Him, and who had been handpicked by His Father God to guide Him until He began to fulfill His great calling to save the world. In that moment on the cross He affirms that the bond between a mother and her son is strong and very much a gift of God. And in that moment He does something prophetic.

Jesus, by dying for the sins of the world, is leaving His earthly home and will now be clinging to His bride, the church. Jesus had left His Father in heaven to find this lost bride, and thirty-three years later He leaves His earthly mother in those final moments on the cross to cling to that bride. The actions quietly inserted here speak profoundly of God's value of the roles women play and the heartbreak we can experience. He identifies with us.

Mary had influence. She was visited by God then carried His Son. She raised Him, knowing He would one day be about His Father's business. I'm sure she wasn't a perfect mother, because Jesus was the only perfect one. And I am sure she was fearful of what Jesus's mission would cost Him and what pain she might endure as His mother. Yet she releases Jesus to fulfill His calling on earth and then to cling to us, His bride.

With compassion Jesus speaks into Mary's breaking heart and gives her John as a son. I think it is fitting that out of the eleven remaining disciples the one Jesus would charge to care for His mother is the one described as the beloved disciple (John 20:2). This John would later pen the Book of Revelation. The disciple who had a deep under-standing of God's love takes care of Christ's mother and then gets to download the vision of His coming kingdom!

These are small insights that have given me such peace about the strength and unique purpose I have as both a woman and the mother of a son. I can choose to believe that I am weak, but that will limit my influence. I am walking a truly amazing road with my eight-year-old son. It is exciting to know I am able to influence him daily, as moment by moment he moves closer to becoming a man. God intended this connection.

We women have great influence in the kingdom. We read story after story of faithful mothers whose influence led to their sons doing great things for the kingdom of God: Moses, Samuel, Elijah, David, Samson—the list goes on. Sons are gifts for mothers to rear, and we can influence them to become who they are supposed to be.

God designed Eve with a purpose in mind. Let's push past all the years we let spiritual blindness deceive us and return to a belief in the beauty of our design. God is still using Eve to direct our steps and lavish us with a knowl-edge that we were made with intention.

There is so much about influence to glean and digest. My heart as the mother of Justice is to simply get better at letting God have all of my heart and direct my steps so that I set the bar for Justice to follow and trust in God as his Father.

Before I had a son, I was in ministry and God had blessed me to be able to lead people into the presence of the Lord. When Justice arrived, even those gifts seemed amplified. I became better at ministering to others as I became better at teaching my own son how to let God love him. This revelation of God's love has become a foundational platform of my faith.

I came to realize not only what the love of God feels like but also how it heals and gives hope. That love moves me to want to be better, walk better, and do life better. It influences me to deeply desire to love others in the same way. Of course, we have the opportunity to give and receive God's love even if we don't have kids, but sometimes the revelation of this truth hits us more strongly as our responsibilities increase. Raising a child is serious business, and it should jar us into asking God more questions about how we are giving our life away instead of squandering it.

Even now that my son is eight years old, several times a week I ask him this simple question before bedtime, "Do you know how much God loves us, Justice?" His response, "How much?" I answer, "More than stars and sky and water in the sea; more than cousins and uncles, aunts, and me. More than the sun and more then moon. He will show us how much when He comes back soon."

Who has had the greatest influence on you? How can you influence the next generation? Influence isn't just for those who physically give birth to children and experience motherhood in the traditional sense. God wants all of us to rise up and believe that what He put in us will come out and that we have been given everything we need in the Spirit to see our dreams fulfilled. We are all up to something, out to be someone, and have dreams we dare to see become reality. We do not need to be mothers to influence. I see young people on staff with me who carry influence simply in how they love and show kindness to those around them.

Showing grace, patience, kindness, and self-control are all big ways we influence others; people see those qualities in us and want to grab hold of them for themselves. We may think the lost are too busy being lost to notice us, but they are watching us as believers more than we realize. People want to be inspired. If you haven't spent much time around true encouragers, find some and watch how they affect your belief and joy meters!

Jesus was the world's greatest influencer. He walked in holiness and perfection, and gave away healing and salvation. Psalm 18:35 says, "You stoop down to make me great." God's influence on us makes us a great people, influencing others by modeling His character.

If Jesus, while dying on a cross, can remember to acknowledge His mother's broken heart in a kind of last kiss, don't you think His thoughts are on you? After all, He left her to cling to you.

8
FINDING WORTH

The days are passing quickly, and though I feel inspired in this new season, I am more exhausted than ever when the daylight ceases. I think often. I sit in quiet times, meditating on God and who He is and who He has called Adam and me to be. I think about these things and know that Yahweh is goodness, and yet there is a strain on my flesh. There are times when I feel I am wandering alone, and I spend moments with thoughts that cannot be from God. I consider how much I love, and yet I feel less love in return. This is not what God desires, for me to feel less loved. My heart questions what should never be put to the test. My flesh puts me to the test. This is the strain of living outside the garden and not being unashamed in our nakedness.

Why do I feel this rush of emotion crashing down on me? There is an invasion in my emotions, and I cannot find the root of entry. I listen for Yahweh to explain, and He speaks of me being emptied and being filled. I would like to avoid this strain, but I cannot. I am aware that as my body makes way to grow another life, I lose restraint in many areas. I feel things so powerfully, even things that cannot be of God. There are moments when I wonder what it would be like to be Adam—all strength and control.

I learn to lean and trust and give away who I am. From breast to hand, my body is giving away everything it can to push life along—though into what I have no idea. Yet am I noticed here in this space? Is it so important to be noticed as Eve, the one who is present here giving birth to life even in my sin? I am not naked but feel at times that I am fully skin. I will meet with God and ask that He find me and speak life. I will seek out Adam and hope for understanding.

BEHIND THE WALLS

She sat in the back of the room when class started just as I expected. I noticed her the night the students arrived for the DIVE worship training school I lead several times a year. She was cool and calm as she scanned the room for exits in case she needed to escape. I could tell she was expectant, but she acted as though she didn't care what happened. She eyed me up and down and without words dared me to get past her walls. I was up for the challenge. All the hurt and shame I had seen while ministering around the world had prepared me to confront another young Eve who had spent most of her time building walls instead of taking them down.

I started praying, asking God to show me how to "notice" her. I firmly believe that women need to be noticed. I see it as a gift. Yes, I said that. I think a woman's need to be noticed is a gift from God. Being noticed creates a strong sense of validation, and when the validation is received and lived out in the way God intended, we flourish as the women we were created to be. The enemy will attempt to distort this desire and make it our great insecurity. It's because of these insecurities that our need to be noticed often works against us rather than for us. But this student didn't need to be noticed because of pride or vanity. Yet this young woman, whom I'll call B, desperately needed me to see her.

B had spent most of her twenties hiding behind walls she had built to protect herself from others. This is because when she was a little girl she had been exposed to a depth of sin that no child should ever encounter. Now all these years later she seemed to have become a professional at hiding in her own dark castle and never letting her draw-bridge down for anyone. Of course, I had no idea where the root of her wounding lay. All I knew was that she was one of twelve students who had come in from across the United States for a week of worship training.

On the first long day of training I made a point to gently touch her arm or shoulder whenever I passed by. It was my friendly way of saying, "I know you're trying hard to be cool, and I see you." B would smirk, and I could tell she was curious to see if I would live up to her expectations of me. She had been a huge fan of my worship recordings, and with so many music artists behaving like prima donnas, she wanted to see if I was the "real deal." In many ways I think she was waiting for me to disappoint her. If I did, she could crawl back to where she came from and nothing would change in her life.

I remember that particular DIVE school starting off with a deep heaviness that I knew was spiritual. By the end of day two I drew the students, who were all women, into a circle and asked them to share where they felt stuck in their lives. Within minutes the women began to tell stories of sin, sorrow, and areas where they felt so bound they could not do anything creative. B was sitting cross-legged on the floor next to my chair. When the women fell silent after sharing their struggles, I looked down and caught B's eyes and told her, "It's now or quite possibly never, girl."

She looked like a woman who'd been caught fully exposed, yet she also seemed relieved. Without much more coaxing, she began to share her story. A male acquaintance of her parents' began raping her at the age of eight. She became pregnant from these encounters at age eleven. She miscarried the baby while at home alone, scared and in shock. During all the years of abuse, she never shouted out or told anyone what was going on because she feared her abuser would make good on his threats to harm her and those she loved. So she endured his abuse until he was arrested when another girl he was abusing cried out for help. This man was convicted and sentenced to prison.

B moved on with her life, learning to wall herself inside and stuff down her emotions and expectations. The furthest thing from her mind was the thought that she had any value. Without hope, she became victim of another pedophile at the age of thirteen and then of a third abuser when she was sixteen. During this time she endured two more miscarriages.

I will never forget that night. After I heard B's story, I remember bending over in my chair and sobbing with grief. I cried because I wanted to have been able to protect her from such horrible things. I wept because I felt she had never really allowed herself to cry. I wept because it made me mad and physically sick to know that someone so precious and innocent had been violated so viciously. I wept also because I felt helpless. I saw her at ages eight, eleven, thirteen, and sixteen shipwrecked by circumstance.

Here she was now in her twenties registering for a little worship school to be encouraged in songwriting and the creative arts, and this became the place where she felt safe enough to unload her burden. I continued to mourn for her weeks after she went home. I don't know that I have ever been so affected by someone else's life. I also don't know that I have ever felt such hope for someone's future. How would any of this—our meeting, her finally sharing her burden—have been possible except for God?

God sees the melody within our hearts and how it sings even in our sorrow. He had been watching B her whole life.

He was desperate for her to hear the sounds of freedom. So He began to untangle her from her shame in those moments at our DIVE worship school.

B told me later that when she was five years old she had an encounter with God that she would never forget. She said an angel came into her room and told her she had been made for "glorious matters." It impacted her so deeply that the experience became an anchor through all the years of pain. The encounter was a ship of hope that she knew was real. Through everything the enemy tried to do to shift her sand, she would remember when God told her she would see glory. She said during the DIVE school that she was finally able to embrace that truth again.

B had an amazing week of release and healing. God was faithful and remained faithful in and through the trials she faced when she returned home. I am amazed and grateful that years later this young woman would be the one to text or e-mail me at the most random times with a profound word from God for my own life. I would be in the midst of something intense and suddenly receive literal words from God written to my heart from her.

I can't think of a better example than B to explain how much value we have as daughters of God. I often wonder how we have convinced ourselves that we do not have value in Christ. I think about the woman in John 8 who was accused of adultery and brought before Jesus. When I read this passage, I cannot help but tune out the voices of accusation and just focus on this woman standing there with Jesus. He does not defend her with many words or even deny her sin. He basically writes in the dust and tells those without sin to cast the first stone to punish her with death.

What He writes in the ground is a mystery, though many theologians have their ideas. Some say He wrote the names of the accusers; others think He may have written those accusers' sins. I have wondered if He wrote something familiar for the woman to read, something only she would understand. Whatever Jesus wrote, I believe the real beauty here is in the redemption. Jesus understood trauma and how it would assault us. But just as He did with this woman caught in adultery, He is in the business of removing our condemnation and handing us back our dignity and hope.

In the last chapter I focused on the influence mothers have on sons. In this chapter I want to encourage daughters. We have so many gifts and attributes, for many of us it will take a lifetime to discover them all. We were made with all we need to accomplish everything God has set out for us to do. We are not inferior to men; rather, we must embrace all the things that make us distinct from them. God made us different on purpose.

I always find it interesting when I see women trying hard to prove they are equal to men. I think this happens because we allow being equal to overshadow the importance of just being. What do I mean by this?

I have spent the bulk of my years in ministry in what is loosely known as the worship music industry. I use the word *loosely* because worship is not really supposed to be a business, but the industry I refer to is one whose primary focus is on creating and producing music that is used in church settings. Despite its aims, positive though they may be, it still is an industry and it often perpetuates stereotypes.

One of the stereotypes this industry promotes is that most worship leaders are men. This was hard for me to deal with for many reasons. In my traveling I have met more female worship leaders than male, yet the role popularly belongs to men. Because of the perception that worship leaders are or should be male, I have had to push my way through a lot of unnecessary debris in an effort to prove myself as a worship leader and be recognized for the gifts God has put within me.

I learned from experience that if I allowed the obstacles in my field to intimidate me, I would limit myself from reaching the potential I was meant to attain. There are plenty of things to be frustrated by, for sure, and there are plenty of obstacles to overcome in life, no matter what field you are in. But only we can prevent ourselves from walking in our calling.

It took me years to realize that I never really needed anyone to validate me as a worship leader because I had God's approval. Realizing that started me down the road of not being affected by what others thought. I have come to believe that my life and livelihood are in God's hands. He opens doors no man or woman can open and shuts doors no one can shut.

I know I am not alone. So often we as women feel as

though we are hitting a wall as we try to get noticed. Our sense of value is attacked from many different fronts—home, church, our friendships, and relational circles. This is why I have prayed for peace about having my gifts validated, and I encourage other women to do the same. We need peace that passes everything we will never understand. God can leave us with a peace so complete that it will keep all of the stress we run up against from preventing us from reaching our purpose in Him.

SEARCHING FOR IDENTITY

Daughters begin learning how to be women by watching their mothers. You do not have to take a psychology course to realize that a distant or distracted mother can cause a daughter to lack a clear sense of identity as a woman. It would be ideal for us to get free of every issue we face before we have children, but that rarely happens. We are all works in progress. Becoming less distracted by our own insecurities would be a good first step toward healing.

The young Eves we birth and mentor need to know they are exquisitely designed and that they have gifts and talents. They need us to tell them all the ways they are beautiful and to hear us thanking God for them. I could not feel the heart of the Lord more strongly for an issue than I do for this matter. If you are a mother of daughters, make a point to thank God for what He has deposited into them—their compassion and mercy, their purity and their passion.

If your daughters wait by the window for their daddies

to come home at night, thank God for their desire to be fathered. And if they are sad that their dad isn't around, thank God for that too, because it is a blessing for them to realize that having a male presence in their lives is part of God's design. They need you to notice them in all their beauty.

Daughters need friends, but friendship is not what they need most from their mothers and mentors. They need wise women who will teach them how to not repeat their mistakes. God is desperately trying to get us as females to love who we are and how He made us. He wants us to know that He is taking notice of us and that He loves the person He made. As we embrace this truth for ourselves, He wants us to raise daughters who also believe they are beautiful individuals with so much to offer. And He wants us to encourage them to dream even bigger and bolder than we allowed ourselves to.

Scripture is loaded with the stories of valiant daughters who came after Eve. I find such pleasure in reading about the heroism of women who understood the deep things of God and fulfilled their destinies and in doing so championed others to do the same. I think of Deborah, a prophetic warrior who in Judges 4 believed God's voice and boldly declared that the battle against the evil rule of Sisera would be won by a woman and not a man. This came to pass just as Deborah had said. Young Jael, armed with only a tent peg, killed Sisera in his sleep. Because of Deborah's confidence in God, others took notice of her and respected her ability to lead.

Anna the prophet was widowed after seven years of marriage then spent the rest of her life in the temple, worshipping God night and day and waiting for the coming of the Messiah. She was eighty-four when a young couple named Mary and Joseph came into the temple to dedicate their newborn son Jesus, in keeping with Jewish custom. Anna saw them and began to speak about Jesus "to all who were looking forward to the redemption of Jerusalem" (Luke 2:38). Anna is remembered in Scripture for her faith. Because she believed God's promises, she was able to proclaim not only Jesus's coming but also His appearance.

In Mark 5 Jesus was surrounded by a crowd, and in all the fuss Scripture makes note of a woman. After exhausting every avenue to find healing for a condition that left her bleeding constantly, this woman decided to seek out Jesus. Amid the throng, she reached out to touch the hem of His garment, and the Bible tells us that Jesus felt virtue leave Him. He asked, "Who touched me?", which seemed like an impossible question to answer in such a crowd. Everyone was touching Jesus, yet this woman's faith got Jesus's attention. She was healed on the spot, ending twelve years of suffering. Her faith had made her whole.

I think also of Mary and Martha, whose brother died of an illness. The sisters knew that if Jesus had been there, their brother would not have died, but He had not come when they needed Him. Jesus knew exactly what He was doing. His actions were filled with purpose. Yet when He saw Mary's and Martha's hurt and pain, He wept (John 11:35). Jesus's purpose was to reveal His Father's glory, but

He also showed Mary and Martha that He noticed them. Jesus raised Lazarus from the dead, and in doing so He showed everyone who had gathered at Mary and Martha's house that He takes notice of our needs. Whenever I read John 11:35, I wonder whether Jesus also wept because His life would also be the next one raised, and no one would be there to see it.

Jesus knows we need to be noticed, and He wants us to know that He sees our faith when we are going through trials. He sees us and wants us to notice Him and feel Him pushing us to move and live and be all we were called to be.

Scripture does not speak literally of Eve's journey with her daughters. I often wonder what it must have been like for them as the ones who would populate the world. And I wonder how differently Eve felt when she gave birth to her daughters. I experienced different emotions when I thought I was going to adopt a little girl than I felt when I received Justice. Before I knew Justice was a boy, I was focused on figuring out how I was going to give a baby girl all she needed to feel noticed and loved, and to be free of the effects of self-discrimination that I had felt.

Eve had children after the fall and after her decision to sin, so she did not raise perfect, sinless sons and daughters. And she likely made many mistakes with her daughters, just like our mothers made with us and that we have made as moms. My mother made many mistakes as she was raising me, but she remained constant in prayer. She was aware that she was rearing six children in a very different environment and season than she grew up in. She did most of that mothering alone because of my father's untimely death. So she sought the Lord to be everything for us that she couldn't be.

When life comes at us, we maneuver through, playing our roles while trying to dodge the effects of the circumstances we find ourselves in. Some do it well while others fail miserably. But everything we choose to deal with or ignore becomes part of the inheritance we leave to our children.

I meet more women on the road than I do men, mainly because I minister often at women's events and because women feel much more comfortable coming up to me after events than do men. For this reason I have seen daughter after daughter describe how their mothers did not know how to love them or tell them they are worthy. I meet mothers who weep while talking about how their daughters hate themselves and have no sense of self-worth. In some situations the fault lies in the way a person was raised, I am sure, but as adults we can turn away from what isn't working and toward what will.

No matter our age, God is in the changing business. It is never too late for Him to teach us how to be, from this point on, better at living as His daughters than we have been so far. When we do this, we cannot just change our own ability to see; we can change the atmosphere of those we have been given to influence. Women, take notice of your daughters, both natural and spiritual, and see how glorious they are.

WOMEN OF STRENGTH AND BEAUTY

I think grace and humility are signs of strength in a woman. Because I lacked a strong sense of good self-worth growing up, I saw myself as weak and invisible. It was not until I learned the art of being humble that I found my strength. What is it about a lack of self-worth that makes it so ripe for the enemy to use to derail a woman's strength?

When I was eight, my father was fighting the battle for his life against cancer. A man my father had met came to camp out at the property we were caretaking. One evening he molested me. Never having experienced anything like this before and having good common sense, I went straight into the house and told my mother what happened. She believed me and had the man sent away, but she never called the police or talked to me about it to explain that the assault wasn't my fault.

My mother was in shock and dealt with her inability to protect me in silence. She was guilt-ridden that she had allowed the man around in the first place. As the saying goes, hindsight is 20/20. At the time my confusion over what happened gave the enemy all the room he needed to plant a seed of low self-worth in my heart. That one incident held enough power over me to distort how I would feel about myself for years.

I forgave my mother for not knowing how much I needed her to be strong enough to talk with me about what had happened. There are things she could have done differently that would have enabled me to still feel worthy and unashamed. I don't think she knew how to do those things. If she had been privy to living out loud and letting her voice rise above a whisper, she might have.

But my mother was a woman of prayer. I believe that while she did not know how to speak life over me, she prayed life. That became essential in my being arrested by the truth years later. My precious mother had enough sense to throw herself at the mercy of God. How do I know this?

At the age of twenty I spent five months caring for my mother when she faced her own battle with cancer. We had many conversations during that time, and I asked her a lot of questions. I was there when she saw the face of God and cried out His name before taking her last breath and leaving this world. The look in her eyes right before she died told me that anything she had missed here on earth, she had finally found. I cannot blame her for what she didn't know to do for me as her daughter. I paid attention to learn what she missed and asked God to fill in the void.

Whether we had great moms or weary moms, strong moms or weak ones, what is most important is that we do not revisit their mistakes. My son, Justice, is black, and I am white. Even in this day and age there are regions in our nation where he is still treated as though he is inferior to others. This breaks my heart as a mother but reinforces my determination to teach him the power of forgiveness and truth, and to know his worth and the way God sees him. The truth will always set us free. He cannot let other people's blindness become the glasses he sees out of. He cannot allow other people's hate to dictate how far he goes.

How we affirm the beauty in our daughters, or any Eve God calls us to impact, comes from what we think when we see ourselves in a mirror. We are all guilty of self-discrimination. We are all guilty of personal failure. We need to awake, arise, and remove the stain of our wrong opinions and believe for a clearer perspective. We cannot give up. We have to keep moving forward and learn to stand tall, carrying ourselves with the posture of redemption rather than bending to the poison of a lie.

Solomon wrote, "If you do not know, most beautiful of women, follow the tracks of the sheep and graze your young goats by the tents of the shepherds" (Song of Sol. 1:8). God is ready and willing to teach us the way to follow. He has not made anything that He didn't fall in love with. It is time for us to believe His opinion of us. It is time to hear Him speaking, "How beautiful you are, my darling! Oh, how beautiful! Your eyes are doves" (Song of Sol. 1:15). Believing God's opinion is what sets us free from being bound to what others think.

My thoughts wander back to my friend and former student, B. When she reached out to Him for healing, God saw B as if she were that woman with the issue of blood in Mark 5. He saw B looking through the crowd and pushing her way past all the men she believed mattered more than she did and were more deserving of what Jesus had to offer. Jesus could feel her fear as she passed by some of those men, knowing she instinctively wanted to run simply because it was a man who had defiled her. Jesus knew that her body had been through enough and she was at the end of the end. He knew she had only one hope left—to touch Him.

He watched as B made her way toward Him then stopped and observed Him from a shorter distance as He spoke words that sounded like life to her. He watched her with His heart pounding and could sense her by His side. Then He saw her make an effort to touch Him, a last-ditch attempt to finally be whole. She reached out and grabbed the hem of His garment and then let it go. In that one touch He felt her fear, her faith, her will to survive, and her weariness. It was met with the power of His divinity and they collided gloriously, like a crashing of meteors. Her broken identity met up with His, and nothing for B would ever be the same.

You see, like B I think we all were made for "glorious matters." If we could only believe that, how our lives would change! Oh, daughters of Eve, will you not believe that this great Father and Husband notices you? He sees the distance you keep and the trauma you live in. He is waiting for you to believe enough in the creative beauty He put inside you to push your way through the crowd and find His gaze. My prayer is that you will find the courage to believe that your weakness can become His strength. You are worth much more than you know.

9
FINDING BALANCE

The sun comes up and goes down, and time becomes our journey just as Yahweh has said it would be. The stillness of night is where I gather my thoughts. I understand peace more in those dark moments as I stare up at the shimmering sky that highlights Yahweh's artistry. Abel came to us on a night just like this. I was not as fearful this time. I understood more, and there was comfort in knowing what was to come. The pain in childbirth is something that continues to remind me of my failing. Yet Adam and I both recognize the grace and mercy of Father in the tiny faces of Cain and now Abel.

Abel is so different from Cain. Cain demands the attention of both Adam and me whenever he is awake. He is solid and sturdy with all opinion and demand. He talks nonstop and even chatters in his sleep. Abel is different. He is soft and content and finds everything he sees as something to smile about. His curiosity makes me stop and look more closely at the details of the world around us.

Cain seems to need to be told he is loved; Abel seems to need to show love. Cain follows Adam hopelessly around, needing to do what he does. Abel is most satisfied knowing where I am and if I am content. I want to remember these moments forever because I feel they are important. I am watching these young Adams change daily, and I realize I am changing as well. I regret so many things even in this short period of time, but I am feeling challenged to not register so much anymore the complaint of my failings. I have spoken with Yahweh about this feeling. He spoke of laying down what would consume my thoughts.

I feel divided at times between my emotions and my spirit's longing to find balance. I am all mother, yet I am all counterpart just as well. My time spent leans much more heavily on the side of trying to figure out how to nurture these young men and find the delight in loving Adam as he deserves. I am aware from watching Adam that he wrestles with the same. There are moments when I feel a loneliness that is not within the Spirit of God. I feel it rise to the defense of my flesh. I know this emotion is not what I am to feel, but I find myself drawn in by the seclusion it offers and the complaint it allows. I breathe in the night air and wait for dawn, because as dawn comes so will the busyness of my duties as caretaker and caregiver. Yahweh, teach me, *find me, show me how to balance it all and walk in the way of gladness.*

BALANCING ACT

Balance has become a favorite word of mine. It is like an umbrella in the rain. It shelters us from the onslaught of stress and pressure that life can bring. Gaining an appreciation for balance is the easy part. Maintaining it is difficult. That takes focus and determination.

Many of us have grown up in households without balance, so it may seem not normal to have appropriate boundaries in life. But I have found such value in making balance part of who I am, what I believe, and how I live life. I stress its need when I teach because it is essential, especially for those in ministry. Women are great at multitasking, but we still have need of balance. Life can get so busy it can make us feel like hamsters on a wheel just trying to keep up.

I have the privilege of serving as one of many pastors on staff at Gateway Church in Southlake, Texas. The staff has been encouraged to adopt a motto: "Be, don't do." That is only possible to achieve when one finds balance. I love one of the dictionary's definitions for the word *balance*: "mental and emotional steadiness."[1] I would add physical and spiritual steadiness to that! Those are the things we need to be constantly monitoring in our lives.

Gymnastics is a sport of balance and precision. It's fascinating to me when I watch it during the Olympics, because I always see it as a picture of the way we need to live. Whether the gymnasts earn a perfect score or not, their ability to even get up on the beam or swing from bars requires radical equilibrium. In much the same way, whether we are working or stay-at-home mothers, married or single, with or without children, we too are trying to master a balancing act!

Jesus had balance in everything He did. He was forever about His Father's business, yet He rested when He was tired. He took time to fellowship. He even wept when He saw His friends' hurt. The balance in Jesus's life is lathered throughout the accounts in Scripture. Yet I'm sure He was aware that in our humanity, we would more often strain in competition with others than live the balanced life He modeled.

Many times we feel stressed out because we don't have balance and are trying to carry a load that is too heavy. Proverbs 11:1 says, "The LORD abhors dishonest scales, but accurate weights are his delight." We find a kind of favor when we walk without excess weight on our shoulders. When our lives are out of balance, we are not able to fully experience the peace and the favor God destined for us to feel. This is a constant struggle, and mastering it is the hard part.

Balance can be threaded throughout our daily tasks and decision making. But becoming aware that balance is needed and valuable is where the journey must start. Balance is knowing what is work and what is too much work. It is not putting too much on your plate because no human can conquer the world in a day. It is setting reasonable goals and not pushing to reach unrealistic finish lines. It is leading and ministering with character and vision but realistically and with holiness. It is being OK that you did not have time to make dinner and knowing that sometimes a Happy Meal makes us happy. For me, it is managing my time so that I don't lack the strength to get the most important tasks done.

In Matthew 11:30 Jesus says His yoke is easy and His burden is light. Throughout Scripture we are warned of the burdens we will pick up if we cannot greet balance with a full embrace. The more we worry, the more weight we carry. Balance is fundamental to making our daily lives begin intentionally and end productively. Women have a tendency to live completely out of control trying to prove we are in control.

Many of us live on the edge of either a breakthrough or a breakdown. Maybe we are trying to prove ourselves worthy and just as strong and full of knowledge as we perceive men to be. Maybe it's because, once again, the enemy knows what God has invested in women, so he sets out to scatter our senses with a lack of balance to keep us from living out the great purposes to which we have been called. I imagine that, just like us, Eve must have felt the need to be the calm in the storm, but she would have faced that with the added guilt of knowing she was the one who brought on the burdens she wrestled with in the first place.

At one time in my life I started seeking God for a balanced way to communicate the truth about His spiritual gifts. You see, I love the gifts of the Holy Spirit described in 1 Corinthians 12. I believe God still gives words of knowledge, heals, performs miraculous signs and wonders, and enables us to speak in tongues and discern spirits. I practice these gifts and have found them to be great treasures in my own life.

Yet I have visited and been part of incredible churches whose beliefs about spiritual gifts, though rich with good intentions, differ widely. Some churches elevate seeing miraculous signs above almost everything else, even the teaching of Scripture. Then there are churches that don't believe these gifts should even be practiced today.

I used to feel very confused about these differing opinions in my youth. I started to find balance when I realized that both groups had a point but neither had found a middle ground. Each side believed their view was the only one that was valid, but both were actually out of balance. This happens in just about every area—from religion to politics to character to curriculum.

I think Jesus brings perfect balance. He helps us avoid going too far right or too far left. I now rely on Him to help me find and maintain balance. For instance, in my humanity I often wrestle with a lack of trust and a fear of failing. I believe God is the healer of those weaknesses, so I have to balance acknowledging my weaknesses without diminishing His strength. I find that balance when I yield to His strength, because His strength will turn to that mistrust and show it the power of God's truth, causing my flesh to bow in surrender. My flesh will always want to be in control, but my spirit pushes to submit to the righteous way, bringing balance in my life.

As truth settles in my heart, it brings calm and renews my thinking. I end up leaving the debris that imbalance breeds at the door of simple truth.

I believe God's truth sets us free. Having balance in your life is part of walking in freedom. Within this freedom a wisdom is dispatched that settles in the "knowing that we know" part deep inside us. This wisdom can cause us to respond differently the next time our flesh wants to rule. Learning truth by reading the Word and devouring its content brings liberty.

I find balance by being aware of my limitations but certain of His limitlessness. I find it when I understand that even when my flesh fails, my spirit can still progress. It is as the father of the demonized boy told Jesus in Mark 9, "Lord, I believe; help my unbelief!" (v. 24, NKJV). This is where I started my journey to find balance. Though I sometimes struggled to believe God's truth, the more I embraced it, the more disciplined I became in many areas of life, from my schedule to my beliefs about God to my relationships with friends, family, and others in ministry.

Those who are in full-time ministry bear a heavy responsibility. That role is not supposed to weigh us down, but at times it can feel that way. God didn't call me to be so busy or stressed out. I put that burden on myself when I confused the priorities I had set for myself with my calling.

Control is an area I have had to find deliverance in. When we struggle with control, we actually run ourselves so ragged trying to take or maintain control that we become more out of control. The perfectionist cannot handle things out of line or out of focus. Sometimes finding balance means you give up what makes you act crazy even if you are convinced it's part of your DNA.

Balance isn't being on time all the time; it's being OK when you're a little late, knowing that you won't make a habit of it. We are so often in a frenzy, and we need to become people of rest and restoration. I once met a young man on a plane. In our conversation he told me all the goals he planned to have accomplished by the end of that year. One of them was to exercise two hours a day every day until December 31. I laughed out loud! I didn't realize he was serious until I began to sense that my laughter offended him. I asked him whether he had made any time for rest. His response to me was, "Rest has nothing to do with meeting a goal."

I couldn't disagree more. Rest, balance, and productivity are best friends. You will not be able to enjoy the goal if you have no strength left after you meet it. I know the discipline of creating balance in my life has protected me from getting sick due to stress or falling into unhealthy thinking patterns that can lead to discouragement, depression, or despair.

I think God intended for Eve to live a balanced life because He knew she would carry a heavy load. As a mother she had the responsibility of caring for children while being a good wife and managing the pressures of life outside the garden. Her life was not unlike ours today. We face intense pressure at work and at home, and we need to feel sure that we are succeeding at all the jobs we have been given. Balance brings that peace.

You cannot spend sixty hours a week working three jobs and not feel exhausted after a while. After creating the world, God rested on the seventh day. That was not because He was physically tired; He did this as an example to us. We need to take time to recharge and renew our strength.

It saddens me to hear of the high number of pastors and church leaders who leave the ministry because of burnout. These great women and men carry a vision and calling to lead the bride to her destiny, and they get so burned out trying to accomplish this that they leave the ministry altogether! Why? The biggest reason is a lack of balance! For some reason we feel that because we are Christians, we have to work for God overtime to get everyone saved, fed, and sheltered.

Full-time ministry takes long hours, and it is taxing, but the most stable churches and ministries are ones that have balance laced throughout their operations and beliefs. I am sure Jesus grew quite exhausted while carrying the sin of the world on His shoulders. He died to pay the penalty for that sin, and then He rose from the dead. I can try to carry the weight of the world, but if I die, I won't rise like Jesus did. I don't need to fight a battle Jesus has already won! He took on the weight of the world so I wouldn't have to.

When I see the rate at which marriages are failing in the body of Christ, I am appalled. How often does this happen because ministry sucked the life out of the marriage? How often is a lack of balance the reason sin has the ability to steal, kill, and destroy? How often do children lose their purity because parents got lazy and stopped setting boundaries around what their kids watched and listened to? The lists go on and on.

My flesh has tricked me into believing that I need to spin that hamster wheel because no one else would take care of the need if I didn't. Perhaps you too have thought, "If I want it done, I will just do it myself." This isn't balance; it's control. After so many years of feeling overwhelmed in life, I finally came to a pretty concrete conclusion. I am not a superhero!

If I don't go to bed at night with the hum of the dishwasher washing away the day's events, the world will not come to an end. If I don't get the worship set list sent until the night before I fly out to the next church, it won't ruin the worship time. If I don't pack Justice's school lunch the night before and iron all his clothes so they have creases, I will not be the world's worst mother.

I can be compulsive about some things. I don't think I was genetically designed to be this way. I think I grew into it because of a lack of balance. I became compulsive because I needed to control what was in my power to manage.

Balance makes us better listeners and better responders. It makes us better communicators and helps us develop the patience to not rush to judgment and to listen before we speak. Balance becomes a vehicle that allows us to find wisdom and remain the calm during a storm. God's truth is the great measuring stick and gives us the right standard to live by.

A Proverbs 31 Woman

On my mother's grave under her name is written "Proverbs 31." She was fully deserving of that label. Proverbs 31 describes the seemingly perfect woman of God, a woman who has "balance" as a middle name. I spent much of my twenties and early thirties trying to be like the Proverbs 31 woman so I could reap the benefits of her diligent lifestyle. It always seemed like I never quite measured up to the greatness of my mother or the standard set by the woman in Scripture! For a while it became kind of an ordeal to even *try* to meet that standard.

Still, my dream was to be *that* kind of woman, following the example set by my mother. My mother had left a legacy so much like the description of this great, balanced woman in Proverbs 31. But for years her shoes seemed too big to fill. I found myself failing in the process, because I did not believe I had any right to be called blessed, virtuous, or someone whose work brings her praise. Yet is not Proverbs 31 included in Scripture to serve as a torch illuminating what is possible if these principles are practiced?

How do we become like this woman, the kind of woman who balances home and health, work and family? This woman was smart, creative, and noble, and her worth was far above great jewels. In fact, Proverbs 31:23 says that even her husband was respected at the gate of the city where he sat with the elders. I mean, to be the kind of wife who brings respect to her husband in his position of leadership—that is some kind of woman.

Proverbs 31 was written by a king quoting his mother. King Lemuel was not a ruler in Israel, and there isn't much written about him except that he had a very wise mother. She first tells him this:

> O my son, O son of my womb, O son of my vows, do not spend your strength on women, your vigor on those who ruin kings.
>
> It is not for kings, O Lemuel—not for kings to drink wine, not for rulers to crave beer, lest they drink and forget what the law decrees, and deprive all the oppressed of their rights. Give beer to those who are perishing, wine to those who are in anguish; let them drink and forget their poverty and remember their misery no more.
>
> Speak up for those who cannot speak for themselves, for the rights of all who are destitute. Speak up and judge fairly; defend the rights of the poor and needy.
>
> —PROVERBS 31:1–9

This mother is telling her son the vices to avoid as king and to remember the poor. It is only after this admonishment that she speaks the famous words about women with nobility. I love the imbalance she presses him to recognize before she tells him that finding a godly wife is worth more than rubies. A man who finds a wife who knows how to maintain a balanced life has found a true treasure.

A wife of noble character who can find? She is worth far more than rubies. Her husband has full confidence in her and lacks nothing of value. She brings him good, not harm, all the days of her life. She selects wool and flax and works with eager hands. She is like the merchant ships, bringing her food from afar. She gets up while it is still dark; she provides food for her family and portions for her servant girls. She considers a field and buys it; out of her earnings she plants a vineyard. She sets about her work vigorously; her arms are strong for her tasks. She sees that her trading is profitable, and her lamp does not go out at night. In her hand she holds the distaff and grasps the spindle with her fingers.

She opens her arms to the poor and extends her hands to the needy. When it snows, she has no fear for her household; for all of them are clothed in scarlet. She makes coverings for her bed; she is clothed in fine linen and purple. Her husband is respected at the city gate, where he takes his seat among the elders of the land. She makes linen garments and sells them, and supplies the merchants with sashes. She is clothed with strength and dignity; she can laugh at the days to come. She speaks with wisdom, and faithful instruction is on her tongue.

> She watches over the affairs of her household and does not eat the bread of idleness. Her children arise and call her blessed; her husband also, and he praises her: "Many women do noble things, but you surpass them all." Charm is deceptive, and beauty is fleeting; but a woman who fears the LORD is to be praised. Give her the reward she has earned, and let her works bring her praise at the city gate.
>
> —PROVERBS 31:10–31

This is a model for us to imitate, but it is more than that. It is not just wisdom for us to learn and live by. It is also a picture of what we represent as the bride of Christ. If you read Proverbs 31 carefully you will see that it is full of mystery and majesty. This woman isn't stressed out and compulsive. She has not turned her life over to exhaustion. She is successful because she is aware of her limitations and concentrates on her strengths. When she sees that her trading is profitable, "her lamp does not go out at night" (v. 18). She gives her attention to that area to make it even more successful.

This woman embodies honor and beauty, wealth and fame. None of her attributes overrides another because she balances the time and attention she spends on each one. She does not stress out about her to-do list because she trusts God to balance her time so that everything gets done right when it needs to.

I do not think that I will ever get to the place of perfect balance. I have never sought to be perfect at anything, just maybe more skillful in certain areas. It concerns me when I see women trying so hard to be better and better, all the while losing the ability to just be. What I do know is that we are becoming a gender who find so much business in trying harder to be better and losing control to just be what we can. The pressure we put on ourselves needs to be released.

This past year I took a much-needed sabbatical. It was my first one ever! In almost fifteen years of ministry I had not taken two months off from traveling in ministry, and I was thrilled with the opportunity to recharge. I had made up in my mind that I was going to rest and restore for two whole months, but taking a break turned out to be the hardest thing I have ever done.

Week one went by fast, but by week three I was over it. The trouble was that I took the sabbatical right after moving to a new state. I had not been able to save as much money as I'd hoped to, so instead of resting, I worried. I worried and worried and worried some more. When my sabbatical was almost over, I still had no idea what rest looked like and felt more out of balance than ever.

I have to give myself a bit of a break. This was my first sabbatical, and I had taken it rather spontaneously in response to the Lord's leading. I may not have taken much time to relax, but that sabbatical did teach me what it means to rest. God showed me that I would never be comfortable with the balance that only He could provide until He became my satisfaction and my true rest. I thought my sabbatical would look like a Hawaiian vacation at which

I was on a first-name basis with a masseuse. Not so. I allowed my soul to thrash around, trying to find a way to bring everything into balance, instead of resting in God and watching Him bring order to what seemed to be chaos.

We need to begin to weed through the chaos in our lives to get to the rest note. I know many women will roll their eyes at the thought that we could even hope to resemble the Proverbs 31 woman. But could it be that we should look at this as a prophetic rather than a literal picture of the kind of bride we are to be? This is not just a proverb full of wisdom. Proverbs 31 is also a prophetic call for the bride to realize her abilities and all her possibilities, and by walking them out with precision and balance, make the name of the great Husband Jesus well known at the city gates.

You are, right now, walking in only what you have dared to believe you could. If that is less than wonderful, it's because you've only believed for less than wonderful.

This is not a perfect world, and we don't live in perfect circumstances. We find candles in Scripture that light the way for us to find the equal but less stressful road. I think Eve might have felt more pressure and strain than we have given her credit for. I also think God showed her how to manage all the tasks she was assigned. Have we allowed God to show us how to do the same?

Maybe it's time to think of pulling back and taking another look at what we are so sure is important that it must be crammed into our already busy schedules. Maybe less is more. Maybe we need to stop long enough to hear the Lord telling us how to be better at being His bride.

10
FINDING FORGIVENESS

Words circle in my mind as I try to make the phrases sound complete. My spirit and flesh are in a collision. I feel as though I am on the edge of a shore. My humanity is standing on one side looking out across to the other side; in between is a body of water that is the flood of my weeping. How do I cross this? How do I make it to the other side of what has occurred under God's watchful eye? I beg Yahweh to reduce me back to the one bone he drew from Adam's side. I beg Him: Let me return there!

Adam came to me with the news that Cain took the life of Abel. This is when my mind went to war and my heart broke in pieces. Confusion sits upon my chest, and I fight every moment to not run like liquid down the mountain. How can I live when Abel will not?

Adam explained in a shaken voice what happened in the field near where Abel tends his herd. Cain had confessed it because God had discovered it. I cannot bear to hear this, and I cover my ears and bury my head in the dirt. Cain and Abel were the beginning of my hope. I had been their witness to life and breath. Cain's resentment I had challenged. His complaint I had warned him to conquer. I had urged him to lay down the myth that God thought less of him and more of Abel.

I cannot weed through this truth yet. My anger rises, and my wailing multiplies. How could he? How could Cain be so selfish to have stolen the breath of his own flesh and blood? I could feel an ugly hate rise as I saw my Abel without breath. Abel, Abel, how you loved to please Yahweh! You were such joy and such contentment to us all. I do not want life without you.

My son is dead and my son has murdered him. Is this not my fault again? I bore this boy in pain, and in pain I release him to death.

I could not look at Cain. He was sent away as I was sent to cover myself in mourning. I understood his agony, but how do I forgive it? I have given birth to a monster. Could not only a monster do this to another human life? How could you, Cain? How could your flesh so need to be validated by God that you would take a life? Yahweh, You stood witness and could have stopped this. Why didn't You stop this?

I am angry, and I am strained. God's voice breaks in to remind me of His words to the serpent in Eden, and I feel it calling me back to fight against this rage. I do not know how to find strength to grieve and forgive at the same time. Isn't that what this will come to?

Forgiveness? I am not You, God! I am not Master of the universe! I am not Spirit alone, like You, remember? How do I hate this sin and not be swallowed by it at the same time? How do I lay this upon Your altar? One man's decision becomes another man's consequence.

Did I nurture this in Cain? This pattern of falling prey to lies is repeating itself. Oh, Yahweh, come! Come to us here because this hate is washing up on shore, and I am in danger of losing my mind to it. You found me in my sin and covered my nakedness and shame. Cain needs the same. Yahweh, show this heart of mine how to forgive.

POWER TO FORGIVE

When I did a Google search for the word *forgiveness*, 54 million results popped up. I think it is safe to say that this topic is one that has many searching for answers. Forgiveness used to be a scary word for me, but I have grown to love it like a friend. It takes patience to understand, but it is critical for moving on through hurt and toward healing.

My desire here is not to give the impression that I can

show you in five easy steps how to forgive. I cannot. What I have discovered, though, is that forgiveness is the key that unlocks many emotional doors, and those doors are worth all the hard work it takes to unlock them. It can bring peace and contentment, and shine light into a room that without forgiveness will always be dark.

There are degrees to forgiveness. If the wound is very deep, it may take a while to fully feel forgiveness's embrace. But it is worth everything it takes to obtain it. The freedom that true forgiveness brings is simply amazing!

Eve was the first woman to have experienced forgiveness. Her sin in the garden was the first offense to ever need to be canceled. So before Adam and Eve exited Eden, God meted out their punishment—and extended forgiveness. The way God covered Adam and Eve after their sin (Gen. 3:21) and provided a cure for sin and death through the promise of the Messiah was a sign of His grace and forgiveness toward them.

God freely forgives us, and He wants us to do the same for others. Forgiveness isn't just about our freedom. The enemy would love to plant bitterness into the middle of a contentious situation and set off an emotional war between everyone affected by the wrongdoing. But the battle to right wrongs belongs to God, and when we give Him full rein to fight it His way, we are able to experience peace. It may seem strange, but I have found that in order for God to take full control and bring lasting freedom, He first confronts me with those I need to forgive.

I wonder sometimes what it must have been like for Eve

to receive God's forgiveness. I'm sure she had to learn to trust herself all over again after she sinned against God. And who knows how long it may have taken her to forgive herself. It's funny, but when we struggle to love others, often it is because we have not forgiven someone. We may be unable to forgive ourselves, or we may be angry at God for something we feel He did or did not do.

I am sure in the course of Eve's life she learned how to take offense and hold a grudge. Cain's killing of Abel certainly would have put her to the test, and the enemy would have been sure to exploit that situation. Satan had been searching for a way to prove the promise God made within the gates of the Eden false. Here was his chance.

Remember, God told the devil there would be enmity between the serpent and the woman and her offspring (Gen. 3:15). In that verse God gave Eve back her power over the enemy with the hope of the coming Messiah, who would crush Satan's head. But the first offspring she delivered was hardly gaining victory over the serpent. Satan, it seemed, was doing the crushing.

Worse, perhaps, was Eve's knowledge that Cain's sin could be traced back to her own. Cain's crime marks the beginning of generational sin. In Genesis 4 we see Cain dealing with the same issues as his parents.

> Then the Lord said to Cain, "Why are you angry? Why is your face downcast? If you do what is right, will you not be accepted? But if you do not

do what is right, sin is crouching at your door; it desires to have you, but you must master it."

—Genesis 4:6–7

Like Adam and Eve, Cain chose to rebel against God. Cain also started questioning his worth much as his mother did. Eve was understandably grief-stricken and angry after Abel's death, but I imagine she may have felt some guilt also. The enemy was never hoping to destroy just Eve. He wanted to destroy mankind through her. Dysfunction is in humanity's genes, but the Messiah has already taken on the offense to set us free.

Life is a series of seconds, minutes, hours, days, and years of learning how to lay down offense and embrace forgiveness. It is the course of humanity to always need to give and receive it. It is health to find forgiveness and wholeness to desire it. Extending and receiving forgiveness can be hard. But those who embrace it find that it is worth more than gold!

Having experienced the embrace of forgiveness, I know I will always need to stay open to forgive and be forgiven. Forgiveness is a pure tool for reaching higher heights and deeper depths in God and with those He puts into our lives. Without forgiveness, I would simply survive, not truly live. I know I need the power of forgiveness to fulfill my destiny. Let me explain.

We all have had people fail us. Many people believe God has failed them. None of us are exempt from walking through situations in life that tempt us to become bitter and unforgiving. I mentioned that forgiveness can be hard. The act of forgiving isn't really what is difficult; it's releasing the person who wronged us that is hard to do.

It can be equally daunting to come to terms with how we ended up needing to forgive or be forgiven in the first place. The circumstances we grow up in or experience in life can cause us to move more forcefully toward darkness than light. We can fall prey to addiction, promiscuity, and other self-destructive behavior. But forgiveness is still within reach, no matter how far a person has strayed.

God extended forgiveness to both Adam and Eve after they made the biggest mistake in the world. Although He punished their betrayal, He also extended to them grace and love. He made clothes for them and gave them roles and duties—a sense of purpose outside the garden. He removed them from Eden but gave them an opportunity to rediscover obedience. God is constant in His forgiveness, and He is constantly urging us to forgive also.

The Lord gave me an insight into forgiveness years ago when I was in a difficult situation with someone who had taken great offense with me. I do not enjoy confrontation, but I found myself in need of confronting some relational issues that I did not want to keep revisiting. I knew that insecurity was at the root of the discord, but trying to reason with this person had become useless. I was always perceived as defensive whenever we attempted to discuss the disagreement.

Communication between us basically had ceased, and, sadly, for me that brought peace. I had been learning to draw boundary lines, and I felt I was doing the right thing and following God by just praying for the offended person rather than trying to mend trembling fences.

Months had gone by, and one afternoon the Lord asked me to send an e-mail to this person accepting all responsibility for the situation that had created the rift between us. I was in shock. I thought I must have heard God wrong. Take on all the responsibility? I had done little to cause the problems between us, and I felt I had thoroughly repented of what role I did play in the situation. But the Lord again asked me to write this e-mail and accept all the blame, as if I was responsible for the lot of it!

I chose to swallow my pride rather than dishonor God, so I wrote the e-mail, all the while thinking I understood why God would have me do this. By writing this e-mail, the offended party would be in such shock that person would recognize I was not the guilty party and then ask *me* for forgiveness. *Yes!*—I mean, great idea, God!

The person responded quickly to my e-mail, and the reply was not at all what I thought it would be. It was a short thank-you for admitting that the fault was mine in the first place!

I was upset with God. He knew my heart was right. Why would He allow the other person to feel righteous in this situation when I was not guilty of what I was being accused of doing? Then God spoke profoundly to me. He simply said, "Rita, I asked you to write that e-mail to show you what I did when I took on all of your offenses. I took all the blame. Without question I laid down My life to set yours free."

I crumbled in remorse and submission. No longer did I think for a minute that I was owed anything in the situation that severed the friendship. My obedience to God in writing that letter broke the power that situation had over me. I had been willing to take responsibility for something I knew I was not to blame for, but I was not willing to play the victim anymore. I appreciated the opportunity to become more Christlike and understand a little better what He has felt.

That experience was the first of several amazing things I encountered on the road to forgiveness. It was at this point in my life that I first felt the powerful effects of forgiveness. I became a fan of it, because I knew I would need it to greater degrees in the years to come.

The Sting of Betrayal

Often it is some form of betrayal that drives a wedge between friends and creates a resistance to forgiveness. Betrayal is a murky swamp of sorrow. It leaves you with deep grief and gives birth to sadness and anger, defense and rebuke. If I had not come face-to-face with betrayal in my own life, I would probably not have recognized its passion to destroy. But it was there in that swamp that God reached down to show me some powerful truths and lead me out into His incredible light.

I found myself caught in a season when I felt the great

sting of betrayal in friendship. I had never before experienced something so intense and so dark. In fact, there were moments when I did not think I could survive the emotional turmoil I was in. I was up against the darkness of anguish, and I needed God to show me how to forgive, because I could feel bitterness invading my thoughts.

I decided that I wanted to be free no matter what it cost, and I wanted that freedom to take deep root in my heart. I was willing to do whatever God asked of me. It did not matter whether others thought well of me or I got my point across. What mattered was that I obeyed God in everything He was asking me to do and that I grew in wisdom. I wanted to respond to the hurt in a way that honored God and Scripture. But I had no idea that the pursuit of freedom would challenge me, change me, and break me in so many ways.

I was praying one morning through some rough issues when God asked me to turn to Matthew 26:47–50. In this passage Jesus is being seized in the garden by His own disciple Judas. Upon Judas's arrival, he greets Jesus with a kiss to show the soldiers he brought with him whom they should arrest. Talk about betrayal!

Jesus knew this was going to happen. In Matthew 26:21 He predicted (in front of the other disciples) that Judas would betray Him. This moment in Scripture is very intriguing to me. Jesus tells this group of twelve men whom He has loved and shown great devotion to that one of them is going to betray Him and another will deny Him (Peter). Both of these men seemed shocked by Jesus's words. Peter denies that he would ever do such a thing, and Judas questions Jesus, saying, "Surely not I, Rabbi?" (Matt. 26:25). After this Jesus breaks bread and proceeds to take Communion with them.

The Bible doesn't say Judas has left the table at this point. So does that mean Jesus identified His betrayer and then broke bread with him? Yes! There at that table before His life is lost on a cross, Jesus has Communion with the man who would betray Him and then speaks words of forgiveness.

You see, Jesus loved Judas just as much as He loved Peter. His hope was that Judas would return and receive that forgiveness. He knew Peter would. God, knowing all things, knew Judas would not. A short time later Judas arrived in the Garden of Gethsemane with the soldiers and greeted Jesus with a kiss. And then Jesus said something extraordinary: "Friend, do what you came for" (Matt. 26:50). Jesus called Judas "friend" even as he betrayed Him.

The morning God showed me that revelation in Scripture as I sat there in prayer listening to God, He parted the bitter waters of my betrayed heart and pulled me out of that deep, murky sorrow. If Jesus could be greeted with a kiss from a chosen follower and still call him friend, could I not do the same if He asked me to? I knew this did not mean that all would be well or that everything would go back to normal, but I could feel compassion evaporating the bitterness I felt. I wept as I continued to think of Jesus that day, looking into the eyes of this man He had gone out of His way to find and mentor.

Jesus sought out twelve men, not a hundred and twelve. He sought out a few good men, and one of them sold out His whereabouts for a few silver coins. Jesus cannot be anyone's son other than God's, because what He saw in Gethsemane was not a man betraying Him but a friend whom He had lost to sin.

I grieved as I realized what probably went on in Jesus's heart in those moments. It was the grief of a rabbi losing His student, a friend losing His brother, and a father losing His son. Jesus had pointed out Judas's betrayal at the Last Supper; symbolically breaking His body when He broke the bread, Jesus offered Judas forgiveness right then and there. But Judas could not receive it and proceeded deeper into the swamp of sorrow, hanging himself not long after his betrayal.

I wondered, "If Jesus shows us that kind of friendship, what kind of friend am I?" Did it matter that I felt justified in my anger and emotionally torn in pieces? Jesus felt the same way. Judas's betrayal caused His body to be ripped open and Him to be wounded for my transgression. The day Christ died, extending to us the Father's forgiveness, was the day He also showed us true friendship.

Even knowing he would betray Him, Jesus still called Judas a friend, and I had to find a way to do the same. I knew this would not mean my overstepping the boundaries I had established or trying to restore what only God could rebuild. I simply knew that from then on I had an amazing example to focus on whenever I needed to choose forgiveness.

Total Release

As God has taught me about forgiveness, I have realized that true forgiveness causes a breaking in our flesh. It affects our character and shifts our will to pursue wholeness. It requires us to let go of our right to feel justified in our anger. A person can focus so long on the scars of a wound that she forgets scars are left when wounds heal. The scars on Jesus's body symbolize the glory of forgiveness.

We may think we deserve to feel our hate and sadness because we have not heard an apology sufficient to release us from our hurt. But we cannot allow our flesh to dictate our season of healing and restoration. I decided I would not allow bitterness to rob me of freedom.

I needed counsel, pastoral insight, and accountability in this season as I sought healing and wholeness, and I did all the necessary homework to succeed in this process of forgiving and letting the hurt go. My pastor encouraged me to read and watch R. T. Kendall's sermon on forgiveness. It was the best, simplest, most powerful explanation of forgiveness I had ever heard. His message brought me such understanding and release.

It was a life-changing season, to put it lightly. Little by little, piece by piece, I laid down all the reasons I found myself drowning in anger and bitterness. I bore witness to all God showed me about myself. I desired to work through everything required for me to be free, and in doing so I could feel the release God was offering me. For me, forgiveness was not about trying to repair damage done; it was also a matter of moving past it.

When it comes to forgiveness we have to do what is required of us without putting demands on others. It isn't always necessary to make sure the party we are forgiving knows how angry we were. If there is still a need to express our pain and write out how we were hurt, that may be a sign that we are still struggling to forgive. It is easier to find forgiveness when we can own any responsibility that is ours rather than putting all our resentment on display and making sure the person we are forgiving sees it before we get free.

My father died of cancer when I was nine. He left behind a lot of baggage for me to weed through. As a child I could not see the freedom that comes through forgiveness; I had only an immature understanding of it. When I became an adult, the enemy was there to tell me of all the reasons I was not worthy of a father and in the same breath he showed me all the blame I should heap on my dad. Instead of finding joy in the time I had with him, I started regretting every minute I spent without my father and blaming him and God for each one of those missed moments.

In time God's love began to expose the areas in my life where I was holding on to unforgiveness because I still believed Satan's lies. The more I let God have control of my life, the more I recognized how much I needed to forgive. And the more I recognized my need to forgive, the more I realized I had been holding God more accountable for my pain than anyone else. God spoke to me on a walk recently and gently reminded me that He is not to blame when people betray us or don't keep their word. He is the promise keeper and will fulfill His words to us no matter what others do or don't do.

We are not in control of what other people do. We are in control of whether we choose to forgive. It's worth doing the hard work to get to the root of what is causing us to hold on to our hurt so we can pull up those roots once and for all and never again mistake them for something we need in our lives.

SHIFTING BLAME

Eve was not at fault for her older son killing his younger brother. Yet Cain's actions caused her to feel great guilt and regret. You see, the enemy isn't satisfied with seeing one person suffer for a mistake. He wants to use those mistakes to put everyone those choices affected in bondage through bitterness. When an innocent person is murdered, the guilty party can be put in prison, but without forgiveness the surviving family will spend their days in a type of prison too. Unforgiveness leads us into deeper and deeper darkness. Forgiveness, on the other hand, has the power to heal even when our flesh is never given the retribution it longs for.

It is understandable that we would want to defend ourselves when we have been wronged. That started in the garden as well. In Genesis 3:12 Adam was quick to blame Eve for their fall into sin. This blame shifting only works against us. It is hard for God to heal what we keep trying to defend. And it is hard to keep trying to defend what God has the right to convict.

Eve did not intend to, but she left us with this struggle. She was human, and it was her choice to deny the freedom that was hers from the day she was created and to believe a lie. After Eve fell, God stood before her, extending His forgiveness, hoping she would reach for it. His hope is that we will reach for it too.

When we are in the midst of a dark season, we cannot always see the escape routes. This is why I am so grateful for time. Time does heal, because it gives us the opportunity to change.

I sit in a field now so different from the one I thought I'd lose my sanity in. I see clearly how God helped me scale walls I had no idea how to climb. I was faced with such hurtful and painful situations I thought they would never heal. When the river of forgiveness flowed, I felt as if my senses came back. In this pasture of forgiveness I hear birds singing instead of counting vultures flying overhead. Now I seek the fullness of constant forgiveness. This is found in gracefully leaning against the perfect shoulder of a perfectly understanding and forgiving God.

Daughters of Eve, let go of what is holding onto your heart and causing you to defend the right to be angry. Let God begin to show you how to forgive and move forward to freedom. I know how deeply wounds can hurt, and I understand how it feels to be betrayed. Releasing offense is hard, but the promise is freedom.

Lay down all your rights to be angry. Give God the hate, the anger, and the resentment, and allow His great love to shed light into those places where bitterness hides. You don't need to seek vengeance; He is your best defense. He is fully aware of all that happened. He knows which roots need to be pulled so you can find new hope and sing the new song. After the Lord brought me through my journey to forgive, He gave me a song. The chorus simply says that it will all be worth it in the end. It will, I promise.

11
FINDING COURAGE

The lines on my face map the way to my past, showing the years since Eden. The pain of Abel's death seems to have buried itself in my heart. My sorrow over having to let go of both sons runs even deeper. Adam and I have been plagued with guilt and remorse. It has been hard to find the courage to not crumble under the weight of all this pain. I blame myself. I see my mistakes like visible stones on the ground. I pick them up and toss them into the distance, but the truth is, they are still there. Out of sight but still there, lying where they landed.

The loss of my sons has been the hardest truth to bear. In Seth I have found renewal. His birth was very different from the others, and Adam and I could feel that there was something different in him from the start. Though he is so much like Adam, he has mercy wrapped inside. We are uncertain of his future, but he has a strength that does not hold back. Seth has been my healing. When I first looked at him, I did not see Cain or Abel, but I felt my heart healing for them both. God in His compassion must have sent Seth to Adam and me to mend our broken hearts.

Of all the sons and daughters born after Seth, I know Seth's conception and birth will always stand out from the others. It was a turning point. His birth reminded me that I must have a brave heart. Not all things are lost. After Seth was born, I stood again. I stood up against a darkness that had come to steal my belief, and I stood to face Yahweh Himself and ask for strength to endure. I am learning more and more about this Spirit that is stronger than this weakness called my flesh. I know I cannot change what has occurred, and I do not want regret to hold me captive.

I am grateful that the seasons change. I long to lay this broken body down and return it to dust as my spirit finds the way home to Eden, as God has said it will. I am not afraid of the end of this life. I long for heaven. I do not know what will occur in the age to come or how my children will respond to the Maker. I can only hope and offer prayers up to Yahweh to remember us and have great mercy on our children and those who come after us.

I feel God's love for us deeply, but what I love most is His friendship and His willingness to commune with us. It has taken great courage for us to believe there is strength in this humanity and that we could partake in His divine nature, which we are in such desperate need of. I believe in a God who is courageous enough to have risked thinking about us and who knit us together in His likeness with the hope that we would love as He does and trust His voice.

I gather my children and tell them this story of God and how He made Adam and me by His hand. I tell them of sin and how it first appeared. Then I tell them who our enemy is. I tell them to be watchful for his attempts to creep into their hearts and confront them with lies. It is my duty to call them into a circle and pray that they seek the Father and Creator, and worship Him only. My last ounce of courage will be used to push them to heights of belief, because I know how easy it is to believe a lie and betray God.

My children also will have to cross those bridges of doubt that sway belief. They will have to be aware that lurking nearby is an enemy who wants to mismanage their dreams and get them to forfeit their belief and trust in God. I have said all I can say. I have prayed all I can pray. I have told them about the great hero God and warned them of how easy it can be to disobey.

Yahweh, I am Your Eve. Do with me what You will. I come washed and clean before Your great mercy and lay my tired bones at Your feet in surrender. Have Your way. Have Your way in me.

COURAGE UNDER FIRE

The word *courage* is tossed around a lot. We use it when we describe people who are fighting a life-threatening illness or those who in a split second saved someone's life in an emergency. We hear it discussed on the news and in talk about heroes of war. It takes a heart of courage to go on the front lines of battle and risk one's life fighting for freedom. The word *courage*, however, should not be tossed around lightly. There is a cost to obtain it. Just as a diamond gets its shape when it comes under pressure, so does courage come forth after a bruising.

Courage is like a muscle you strengthen in your core. Building the muscle will help stabilize your spine, but it will also leave you sore. No pain, no gain, as the saying goes. In a race, most runners look toward that finish line, with their sights set on the reward they will receive when they cross it. But they must first find the discipline to train. That takes courage, just as it takes courage to fight the odds and live a righteous life.

The dictionary defines *courage* as "the quality of mind or spirit that enables a person to face difficulty, danger, pain, etc., without fear; bravery."[1] In Scripture the word *courage* is often used in reference to bravery. When God called Joshua to lead the people of Israel into the Promised Land, he told him to be strong and courageous (Josh. 1:6). Throughout the Old Testament God told the Israelites to take courage as they went into battle against their enemies.

But one of my favorite references to courage is in Matthew 14:27. After Jesus fed the five thousand, the disciples went out in their boats and began to fight the currents. They saw Jesus walking toward them on the water and immediately thought He was a ghost. But Jesus told them, "Take courage! It is I. Don't be afraid." I find this account both moving and humorous. Jesus defies the laws of physics by walking on the water, modeling for us the courage to walk by faith. Yet in the same moment He has to tell His disciples to find the very courage He is modeling just to believe He is who He says He is!

Jesus Himself embodied such bravery throughout the New Testament and displayed the ultimate courage when He died for our sins. In fact, in the Garden of Gethsemane He sweat blood because of the great task that lay ahead of Him. Only courage and His Father could have empowered Jesus to complete His mission.

In His innumerable acts of bravery—from healing a man on the Sabbath to defending a prostitute in public to casting demons out of a man who had terrorized a community—Christ shows us how to take heart and be more like Him. He was up against life's circumstances, just as we are. The Bible says He was tempted in every way we are, yet without sin (Heb. 4:15). Our God *is* courage, which raises an important question. If God made Adam and Eve in His image, wouldn't His courage have somehow been transferred to them?

As I was writing this book, examining Eve from all angles, I kept hearing the Lord use the word *courage* when describing her. In fact, I now see her as being far more brave and courageous than gifted or beautiful. To see her in this way we must look past her sin. You see, the only thing we have ever read about Eve is her sin, but you find there is much more to her when you search for her heart. It does not take courage to sin. It would, however, take courage to survive the aftermath of that sin.

It takes courage to give birth and raise children without a road map. It takes courage to toil to survive. It takes courage to believe God could still love you after you'd made a life-altering mistake. I know many teachings out there focus on Eve's mistakes. But the truth is that Eve must have had true courage to face what she encountered!

We have all had to deal with the consequences of our bad choices, but hands down Eve had it rougher than we could ever imagine. This woman was never a child. She was not the baby or the young girl we once were; she had no mother to show her the way. She manifested out of the heart of God. She was the product of the thoughts of God Himself. He had an idea and stepped forward to shape it. The result was Eve. She was not given the same opportunities as we were. We had the opportunity to learn and mature over time; she had to learn day by day.

Eve was the first; it would have been easy for her to fear what was to come. She needed courage to overcome the pressure of the flesh to give in to fear, doubt, and the sin always crouching at her door. How do you gain and lose and lose and gain without growing in courage as a result? Perhaps if sin had not come into the picture, courage would have looked like strength. But because of the fall we, like Eve, need courage every day just to overcome sin and survive the sorrow a fallen world can bring.

My friend Marie Monville knows all about this. She

had to quickly pull up brave bootstraps in 2006 when her world turned upside down. On October 2 of that year police descended on Marie's doorstep and informed her that her then-husband, Charlie, had taken an Amish schoolhouse hostage and stolen the lives of five young girls before killing himself.

Marie needed great faith, hope, and courage to sustain her when despair threatened to bury her in darkness. She e-mailed me sometime later and told me that my music had held her hand through much of that dark time. I was undone, especially when I learned that we had met years before when I was walking off the stage at a conference she was attending. I stopped to pray randomly for her then two-month-old daughter. Only God knew then what Marie would one day face, and He knew the strength He had placed inside her.

In the aftermath of that tragedy Marie found out how brave a heart she had been given. She discovered how kind and big God's heart toward her was, and how He longed to rescue her. She learned that where darkness visits, God will set courage in hearts to light the way home.

I know a young couple who has suffered five miscarriages; the last one was on their anniversary. These two are young God lovers who believe with all their hearts in the promises of God. They hold tightly to every word and prophecy they have received about having children one day. It is this young wife who less than a week after losing her fifth pregnancy organized meals for another friend who had just given birth to healthy triplets. This young woman delivered kindness even though she carried inside a grief that ran down to her bones.

Recently my young friend was at a party that another friend of hers was attending with her newborn baby. My grieving young friend walked over to that mom who was celebrating the arrival of her third child and, with permission, wrapped that newborn baby in her arms. Maybe she was trying to be bold and fight off sad thoughts. Maybe she was trying to push through her pain by getting on with her life. Or maybe—just maybe—she was again acting courageously to heal her soul.

You see, it would have taken courage for this young woman to set up those meals for her friend who sailed through a pregnancy with triplets while her own uterus kept rejecting pregnancies. It took courage for her to stand up in a crowded room and hold that newborn baby, and smile and genuinely mean it.

We are capable of strength and capable of being brave. I imagine that this strength was available to Eve in the beginning much like another choice. Have hope or live without expectation. Pick yourself back up or live in failure. These were the options available to Eve, and they are the choices we continue to face.

Courage must be found relevant in our faith today. How many times have we read or watched a story of heroism and not felt life and gratitude begin to rise within us? How much more will a story with a heroic ending leave us with a sense of hope and the power to prevail than one where all is lost? Courage is like a match that is struck to become a flame. With that match of courage, a fire of belief can be lit in a perishing heart.

Years ago, when I would feel deeply overwhelmed and could literally feel darkness and depression knocking at my door, the Lord gave me a clear strategy to fight it off. I would simply ask Him to show me the faces of two or three people I could encourage that day.

Without fail, the Lord would answer that prayer. I then would dial their numbers or send them a text or e-mail sharing what I felt God wanted me to encourage them with. This small bit of encouragement sent my own darkness fleeing. It did not matter if I was waiting for answers for my own life. Sending out those encouraging thoughts to others was like a spark that lit up my faith and gave me the strength to keep standing as I waited for God to meet my own need.

Our enemy is most afraid of our belief. This trust and strength comes only from leaning on a strong God. If we stand on a faulty belief system that is not deeply rooted and grounded in truth, then we are doing little more than putting on an act rather than developing strength the next generation can learn from. There are ways to *act* courageously and ways to *live* courageously. The key ingredient for courage is a heart willing to be truthful and righteous. We set a pattern of truth for ourselves based on what we choose to believe.

Without the willingness to step out, I think I'd always be wondering what could have been if I had risked my heart to believe or my voice to speak out or my prayers to be offered up. I wonder how anyone can live without ever feeling brave.

A bride looks the most beautiful when she is standing in her white dress with her hair and makeup set, ready to walk down the aisle. This is when she is recognized as the bride she is. To her husband, no other woman compares to the bride in that moment. To me, stepping out in courage to act like Christ makes us look like that bride in the white dress: radiant and lovely.

Stepping out in courage can set our hearts on a course to find the strength to love and hope. Courage does not take the "get out of jail free card"; it does not walk the easy road. I have watched society work very hard to get the church to change its mind about what the Bible says is sin and accept everything as permissible. It concerns me to see how few within the body of believers are willing to stand up to speak truth in this secular culture—without judgment but truth nonetheless—because they fear being disliked. Courage is not just found on battlefields and in war zones. It now can be found among those simply willing to stand up for righteousness.

All lifestyles are not the same. Eve was created by God to be with a man. God did not give Adam another man as his helpmeet. Nor did He provide an Eve for Eve. He put male and female in that garden to set a precedent of what He desired to see among mankind. The only way we can debate this is if we do not believe in God's design and purpose for our lives. The lost are lost, but when the church ignores what the Bible clearly proclaims to be true, it breaks my heart. It will take courage to stand for righteousness and truth and discard the lie that is longing to consume this generation. As truth gets drowned out by the multitude of voices in this media-saturated society, we need to find courage now more than ever.

In Pursuit of a Holy God

Eve was not created only for the purpose of tending to Adam. They were both created to give honor to a holy God who was the reason for their existence. Eve had a choice just as we do, but I believe she thought of Yahweh more often in a few seconds than many of us do all day. It would seem that when Eve cried out to God she did so because He was such an integral part of her belief structure. How could she not have thought of Him? Again, Adam and Eve certainly had distractions, but they did not have the kind of distractions we have today, the kind that derail our commitments and devotion to God. Even after the fall, they must have had such close communion with God compared to what we often experience today.

When we read these scriptures in Genesis, we get a glimpse of something much deeper than meets the eye. The more I commune with the Lord, the more I desire communication from Him and the deeper I feel drawn to Him. I can only imagine what it would be like in my limited knowledge of God to commune with God the way Eve did. She had an understanding of His deity from a perspective that we will not truly have until eternity hems us in.

God was to be honored then as much as He is to be honored now. God reached down to dust and then reached in for bone for the sake of creating relationship and required from those created beings worship and obedience. Adam and Eve were made to worship something, and God's hope was that they would find Him the one to honor and worship.

Honoring God with our worship is primary in our relationship, and sin is the only thing that came between man and God then and now. Our issues have not changed much. We just have more obstacles now because the flesh has continued to convolute the simplicity of worship and honoring God. Perhaps the sin Eve allowed herself to fall into amplified areas of weakness that resided in her all along, blinding her to the strength knit within her.

I am looking at Eve when I look in the mirror. I am aware that through God in me I have what it takes to overcome the insecurity and the way of sin. He knit me together with the ability to succeed, yet when I gaze at my own failing and am persuaded to believe a lie, I see only weakness. I do not see myself with a brave heart because I am too busy mourning my weak and broken one. To me, courage is something we should value enough to know where its reserves are located within us. Hope is what tells courage to arise and believe.

I doubt Eve would have walked around feeling pride for being the first woman created. She had been challenged by life's circumstances, and people in the middle of a trial don't usually walk around thinking they are amazing.

Times of testing (and just living in general) press us into the people we are. Maybe it was in those raw first years that courage was birthed in Eve and then placed as a seed in the hearts of all of us who would come after her with a note that says, "You will need this to survive." I picture Eve falling down the rabbit hole of life and discovering in it the Father's heart by drinking in His courage. Courage, then, is her legacy to us.

In the Scripture verses that follow Adam and Eve's era we see that David found bravery fighting off lions and bears and courage killing a giant. Deborah found courage to go with Barak into battle. Daniel was courageous enough to keep praying to the Lord despite the king's edict. He ended up roaming in the lions' den as a result, but God protected him. Shadrach, Meshach, and Abednego knew courage while standing in a fiery furnace and not getting burned. Mary the mother of Jesus found courage by trusting in God, whose ways were beyond her ability to comprehend. Esther found the courage to do what she never thought she could: risk her life to save her own people. In finding courage, we find favor with the King of kings, and with that favor kingdoms are saved and lives preserved.

Psalm 1 says, "Blessed is the man who does not walk in the counsel of the wicked or stand in the way of sinners or sit in the seat of mockers. But his delight is in the law of the LORD, and on his law he meditates day and night. He is like a tree planted by streams of water, which yields its fruit in season" (vv. 1–3). How can we be like trees planted by springs of water? We get there by obediently walking, standing, and sitting in righteousness, ever meditating on the Lord's truth about us. It is then that we grow to produce fruit that encourages fruit in others.

Think of Esther. Even today how many women has she inspired with her willingness to be brave and step into her calling by stepping out of her fears? Courage is part of our DNA. It is knit in there along with knowledge and choice. I believe it is there not just because it is some kind of spiritual gift but also because Eve needed it to move past her flesh and into the will and wonder of the Lord. Adam and Eve's bloodline carries enough generational sin to weigh us down for our lifetime. Yet in those same bloodlines there must also be generations' worth of courage ready and waiting to be reborn.

I have had countless conversations with women who say they are envious of my relationship with God. Most of these women don't realize what it costs to walk closely with God. They look at the fruit without seeing the cost. We look at mansions and see their beauty and envy those who can afford to live inside. But we never stop to think about what it cost to build and then maintain those mansions. Having depth in your walk with God is the same. It is built through commitment and follow through, not drive-by prayers in the busyness of the day.

Eve had depth. I truly believe this. How could she not? She had questions and quandaries and challenges pressing her on every side. She must have had a deep relationship with God to have stood in faith through them all.

For me, it takes courage to be a single mom. I don't

want to raise Justice alone, but until God provides a stellar natural father for him, I must. This season for me has been harder than the last one. When I was single without a child, I had myself to look after and work on. Now it is not just myself; I am responsible for another life and for influencing how he believes and trusts in the Lord.

As Justice grows older, he is becoming aware of boundaries and the consequences of crossing those lines. And he has become more inquisitive. No longer is he satisfied with what I tell him "because I said so." Now his comments have more "whys" and "how comes" in them. Often I feel that most of what I tell Justice is floating in one ear and out the other. I can only hope his spirit is retaining some of what I say. I feel worn out most of the time...and alone. It is a walk of faith and courage that every single mother takes to raise her kids with godly wisdom and understanding.

It took a brave heart for me to adopt on my own. It will take a brave heart to continue raising Justice on my own. That kind of bravery produces faith because as a single parent I am trusting a Father and a Husband I cannot see with human eyes to lead us. And I am trusting myself to hear His voice speaking, "This is the way, walk in it."

Trusting that voice builds faith, that faith gives way to hope, and that hope lifts up a song in worship. This is my life's cycle: brave belief and faithful, hopeful worship. Courage is not a perfume you spray on the outside; it is the scent of the Spirit coming from within.

It takes courage to want to live through divorce and

tragic circumstances that can cause you to doubt God's goodness. I think of my precious sister who was left to pick up the pieces of her life after divorce. She thought she had a good life but now must find courage to build a new one.

In finding Eve we have to find courage. We must look supernaturally to see Eve's courage without knowing much about the daily routines of her life. As women we can relate to her having to push past doubt. But it would take a brave Eve and a heroic Adam to not hold themselves captive to their sin even as they found traces of it in their son's murder. Courage would take them through every possible turn—just as it takes so many of us—to rise above life's circumstances.

The birth of Seth was a reawakening for Adam and Eve. From Seth's lineage would come Noah, whom God would use to start over when mankind's wickedness became too great. God would find from the loins of Seth one who wanted God completely, and He would start the world over again with one man's courage and brave heart to stay devoted in a wicked world.

Women of valor and courage are not as hard to find as we may think. We demonstrate courage daily without registering that it, indeed, is just that. We often think of courage in terms of acts of heroism. But we are modern, everyday courageous people who push through what life hands us and make choices each day to act courageously or feel defeated. How can we see ourselves more as God sees us? I cannot fathom that God did not knit in me everything I would need to handle all I would face. So let me encourage you with this: He has given you what you need to stay in the fight.

I am in constant awe of how many women in the church do not encourage one another. What causes us as women to neglect to encourage the gifts in others? Is it because we live in fear of someone else being noticed instead of us? Why must we live in competition instead of complimenting the gifts in others? I see this over and over, and it stuns me because I live so far on the other side of the spectrum.

I spend so much time shoveling courage onto broken, wounded hearts that I sometimes have no patience for those who cannot see the glory in how this all works together. I have seen the benefits and beauty of encouragement, so I keep shoveling. In fact, I would much rather encourage than ever be encouraged myself.

I longed for years to have an older woman in the field of worship to mentor me in my gift. I needed it. I prayed for God to send me an elder in the faith who would see my gift, call it out, and wrap life around all the insecurities I felt. No one did. This was hard for me to accept. I would be around so many talented older teachers and singers, and not one of them was willing to take the time to wrap life around me. I spent years thinking I didn't have what it took to be good at leading worship.

Then one day while I was still in ministry school, I received a word from a prophetic speaker who came in to teach. He spoke to me about my need to be noticed and encouraged, and told me that God approved of me and through Him I would learn how to encourage others. I made a decision then to never walk away from an opportunity to throw courage on someone who needed what I realized I may never receive for myself.

Insecurity will always drive a wedge against our ability to be an encouragement. For years I could believe in others but not in myself. Although I longed for a mentor to help me break free of that insecurity, the truth is that no one but God could ever have healed that place in my heart. That doesn't mean I didn't need encouragement.

God wants to use us to throw life on one another. His desire is that we learn how to raise one another up and not drag others down. The power of life and death is in the tongue (Prov. 18:21), and words of affirmation and life can cancel the assignment of words of death.

How many of us have spoken words of death on others out of our own insecure need to have our own gifts noticed? One weekend I was leading worship for a women's event that featured a speaker who was fairly well known. I was blessed by her message and made sure to tell her this when we were back in the greenroom. When I complimented her, a wall seemed to go up, as if it were hard for her to receive this from me.

Speakers aren't usually negative to me at women's events, but it was obvious that it seemed painful for this person to acknowledge me in any way. I felt a spirit of rejection hit me automatically. Back at the hotel I prayed about what I was feeling because it seemed so juvenile to be feeling this way. I had great security in what God thought about my gift. I didn't know why I was even remotely concerned with what this speaker thought.

The next morning I led worship, and the Lord showed up and blessed us with His presence. When we concluded the worship time, this particular speaker got up and proceeded to thank everyone who helped make the conference a reality. She even asked for a round of applause for the sound system crew—the sound system that was so poorly run we had to fight all weekend with various problems. She mentioned everyone *except* the worship team.

I sat there vexed. What was her problem? Who did she think she was? I started to ask God why this bothered me so much. Why was she able to make me feel so unimportant? I began to repent for my resentment of this woman I didn't even know. I repented for needing her approval, which was kind of silly anyway. Then I asked the Lord to show me if this was my issue or hers. I asked that He force her to pray for me if this was an issue she was dealing with. *Force her!* I know it sounds silly, but that's what I prayed for.

At the end of her teaching I came up to play piano for her during the altar ministry. To my shock she turned around and with what seemed like exasperation declared that she should pray for me. I had to smile, because in that moment I felt so grateful to the Lord for giving me a desire to encourage. I do not have to be forced to pray for or encourage anyone. I do it because I love to see in others what Jesus does.

I felt compassion for this speaker, who seemed to have it all together on the outside but obviously battled insecurity on some level. I was relieved in many ways after she prayed for me and unsettled in others. I wondered how it was possible to encourage in one moment then discourage in the next.

I see this all the time among women. We battle the enemy's lies all day long, and most of us don't even recognize it. Women have incredible ability, insight, and revelation. We need to use these gifts to set encouragement in the hearts of others!

Eve's Redemption

I found a place in Scripture in which I was able to see for myself how courage can be carried down through the ages and handed to us like a victory baton. Without a doubt Adam and Eve were the firstfruits of God's vast creativity, and they were fashioned with His great affection and love. Yet as I wrote the words of this book, trying to understand Eve and trace a path to her redemption, I began to wonder, "What does Eve's redemption look like for us?" Then the thought hit me: If all of us are capable of making the same mistakes she did, are we not also able to amend those mistakes or at least not make them over and over?

At times it seems women watch the kingdom of heaven advance from the nosebleed section while the good seats are given to men. That isn't actually true, but it feels that way sometimes. At one time I may have been concerned by that, but now I have peace knowing the Father sees me and that for Him position comes to the humble not the proud. That is because I see how God brought Eve's redemption and caused her courage to flow down to a generation like ours.

There is an unlikely woman I found in Scripture to whom this redemption comes. Her name is Mary Magdalene. I love the fact that in the last few moments of Christ's life, when He is on the cross, He is surrounded by women, one of them being Mary Magdalene. Then in all four Gospels Mary is there at the burial tomb of Jesus along with several other women. This woman's encounter at the tomb paints such a beautiful picture of the redemption of Eve.

Mary found healing in the knowledge of the Messiah. Scripture says she was delivered of seven demons (Luke 8:2; Mark 16:9). Somewhere in this woman's troubled life she comes in contact with a redeemer who not only delivers her of oppression but also in that deliverance shows her unconditional love. After her deliverance, Mary seems to constantly be where Jesus was. She does not seem to need to be pointed out, she is not taking center stage in the accounts, but Scripture lets us know she is there, again and again.

This to me points to her devotion, dedication, and gratitude to the Lord for healing her. She watched and listened, taking in all Jesus said. She became a witness to how He healed and stayed with Him through His crucifixion and His burial.

In John 20:1 we see Mary going to the tomb where Jesus

lay while it was still dark. She finds the stone rolled away and runs to tell Peter and John that someone has stolen the Lord's body. Peter and John come to see for themselves. John races Peter there to find that, indeed, the tomb is empty. The disciples cannot see the foretelling of Scripture yet. They leave brokenhearted, and Mary Magdalene stays and weeps over the loss of her friend, Jesus.

Then she peers back into the tomb and sees two angels seated where Jesus had been, and they ask her why she is weeping. She begins to explain. She is distraught by Jesus's disappearance, and as she describes her sorrow, Jesus appears and stands before her, but she mistakes Him for a gardener. Through her tears she is asking Jesus, without knowing it, where His body has been taken, frantic to know where her Lord is. Then something changes in John 20:16 when Jesus says, "Mary."

He simply speaks her name. Here is a woman who would have come from the line of Eve, just like us. Her life was not perfect, and it is obvious that she had been exposed to some intense heaviness because she needed deliverance. The result of that deliverance caused her to devote her life to this one named Jesus, who spoke truth that she was in desperate need of. She is the most unlikely candidate to first announce the resurrection. She did not come to the tomb that day to announce an awakening. She came to mourn the One who had awakened her.

What we see is God reaching all the way back to Eve in Genesis 3:14, where He told the serpent that One would come who would crush his head. While God's Son, Jesus, is being raised from the dead, He is also crushing the head of the serpent that brought Eve to her place of sin in the Garden of Eden all those years ago. It is fitting here, then, that Mary even mistakes Christ for a gardener.

This time there was no hiding from God. Jesus is standing before Mary, redeeming Eve in the process. This woman who would appear to have no right to be the first one to see Jesus is, in fact, the one He chooses to proclaim His resurrection back down the mountain to the disciples. Eve was deceived way back in another garden and was given a promise that the same enemy who deceived her would get crushed one day. That one day arrived, and it was shown to a daughter of Eve. In this powerful redemptive moment the promise to Eve is fulfilled, and Mary is the one to witness it.

How profoundly is this prophecy in Genesis made clear in the Gospel of John. God fulfills a promise to a woman deceived in the beginning of the Old Testament by revealing that promise to a woman in the New Testament who had once been taken captive by the enemy herself and had received deliverance.

When Mary Magdalene finally realizes who Jesus is, she cries out, "Rabboni," or "Teacher." In that word she acknowledged herself as His student, His lesson once again healing her heart.

For Mary Magdalene it took courage to believe there was more to life than being possessed by something other than truth. It took courage to receive deliverance. It took courage to believe in a Savior. It took courage to watch

Him bleed on a cross, and it took courage to make her way to the tomb to grieve His loss, only to find that He was alive. Oh, to have that kind of courage to experience such amazing redemption.

I love the Lord. I love the audacity of the hope He brings.

Are we not somehow all hidden heroes waiting to appear on the scene, giving courage to others? Are we not all capable of evangelizing not just with our voices and our gifts but also with our hearts and our hopes? Can we not all relate to grief and sadness or the need to be healed? Mary Magdalene came many daughters after Eve, and within those generations of women the battle to believe sometimes came at a great price.

I love that picture of a once demon-oppressed woman who was delivered by Christ—this Jesus Christ whose Father God pulled a bone from the side of man many years before and made a promise to young Eve that out of her sin and regret redemption would come.

There on a hill outside a tomb with the stone rolled away redemption shouts its way down a mountain declaring, "He's risen from the dead! He did it! He crushed the head of the serpent in that garden called Eden." He is a God of His word and a redeemer of those He loves.

Daughter of Eve, we don't have time to waste on our insecurities. We should not be so worried about being recognized for our gifts and talents that we cannot champion those around us to shine brighter. We are women of wonder and purpose, and we have so much to accomplish. We need to find our fractures and heal before we leak our insecurities out over everybody around us. We need to find courage and carry it as constant hope that we will find more courage when we find more of Christ.

Acts 17:26–28 says, "From one man he made every nation of men, that they should inhabit the whole earth; and he determined the times set for them and the exact places where they should live. God did this so that men would seek him and perhaps reach out for him and find him, though he is not far from each one of us. 'For in him we live and move and have our being.' As some of your own poets have said, 'We are his offspring.'" When we live and move in Him, He becomes more of our security and we become less insecure. He increases; we decrease.

Eve received a promise that God had put enmity between the enemy and her and her children. After His resurrection Jesus looked into the eyes of a woman much like Eve and let her see those ancient words finally be fulfilled. It is a gift from God for a woman to have been there at that tomb. It is like a kiss from Him telling us that He sees through our skin into our hearts and He knows how to redeem. He hands Mary Magdalene in John 20 the courage He promised Eve in Genesis 3. Courage is raw, it is beautiful, and we need it more than we know.

In my relationship with the Lord what I long for the most is to one day hear His voice simply say my name. I wait for that moment more than anything else. Then I myself will cry, "Rabboni." He is my great teacher. "Wait for the Lord; be strong and let your heart take courage; wait for the Lord!" (Ps. 27:14, esv).

12
FINDING EVE

I prop my aged body up to rest against this tall, strong tree in this place I have so often come. This tree must be as old as I am, but it will outlive me in so many ways. These old bones of mine seem to bend my body toward the ground more and more each day. So appropriate I suppose. These bones came from the dust shaped by Yahweh's creative hand. Why should I be surprised that they would long to return there? In this silence I hear my own labored breathing. I am at the end of one thing and the beginning of another. I sing under my breath the same tune I have sung when I have felt the presence of the Almighty the way I do now. I struggle to my knees and lay down upon my face, ear to the earth.

Yahweh is good. I lie in remembrance of what the years have brought and what I have suffered by wandering from

His goodness. I do not deserve His attention, but He has thought of me. He has known all that was, and He knows all that is to be. For His knowledge of my life and the shaping of my bones, He is good. He is everlasting, and I am undeserving but ever so grateful for breath and life and His finding me.

Back in the garden when I had strayed, He looked for Adam and me. He asked, "Where are you?" We answered hesitantly, not knowing what to expect. He looked for us, and we came to Him. I did not know then just how lost I truly was. He kept looking for me—when I was buried in sorrow and disappointment, when I was longing to know where and how I fit, He just kept looking. And He has found me—and I have found Him. In His eyes, I see Eve.

I am weak and frail and yet full and found. I am not perfect, but I was able to stand beside Him who is perfection and gaze upon His brilliance. I was not the Eve I could have been, but I did my best and offered myself back to Him. It is this offering that He recalls to me. He kept no record of my wrongs. I am His first daughter, and He is my only Father. He is the One who sat me next to a man and found me when I ran hiding. He is my teacher and my coach. He is my great deliverer and the deliverer of the fruit of my womb. He is grace, and grace has led me home.

I suspect when I leave here that Yahweh might take me back through Eden. Maybe He will let me stop before that center tree. Yahweh and me together once again in Eden, the way it should have always been. Joy then will come; I *sense this deeply. I am no longer in need of proving that I have a future despite the sin of the past, for this time heaven is my future, my destiny to come. I sigh and turn this old crumbling body over to stare at Yahweh's sky. I raise my hands to reach for Him. I reach for this great, patient, wonderful God. I am reduced to one effort and one desire—to never let Him go.*

I water this patch of dust with tears that become my simple worship. The earth soaks them in with great welcome. My last offering, perhaps.

SEEING EVE IN A NEW LIGHT

I went on a search to find this Eve in Genesis after hearing the Lord speak about the mystery of her life. It began with conversations about myself: Why I repeated the patterns of my insecurity. Why I allowed the disposal of my faith when storms rattled the windows of my heart. Why the desire to be noticed seemed to come with such demand and then such denial. I had been asking the Lord so many questions about myself, and He brought me to the beginning, where He spoke to me about Eve.

He spoke, and I listened as He began to show me why I struggled to believe I was fearfully and wonderfully made. I began to see where the fractures in my faith lay as a woman and, more importantly, as a daughter of God. I also had no idea that I would be led on a journey to see Eve differently than I ever would have thought. I did not find a woman weak and lacking. Quite the opposite, actually: I found a role model for all the women who would follow her.

Eve lived in a different time, but like us she was under the watchful eye of a God who could never stop loving what He created and never regretted what He made. The hope He had for her is the same hope He has for us and every other daughter who will follow. God did not make anything that He did not desire to lavish His love and goodness upon.

Adam was the first male, handcrafted by the Father, and out of that wonder God took a rib and created someone to walk beside him. This extravagant act of creativity comes from a divine Father who longs for us to choose Him, just as He longed for Adam and Eve to choose His way. He wants us to follow Him, and in so doing choose to be a part of heaven's sound of worship and Eden's hope, which is Satan's defeat.

Adam and Eve failed in this early on, but through God's grace and mercy they were reshaped by His kindness to rule and reign despite the heaviness of their sin and the detouring of their faith. God recaptured their hearts and gave them a way to find life outside of Eden. God knit, He named, He gave, and He grieved over these two beautiful beings with whom He longed to share His heart and live in friendship.

When you set off in search of something, you may find more than you bargained for. I know I did. I began my search with a sense of purpose. I felt the Lord stirring me to seek out Eve. There are so many more truths about her yet to explore. But I have attempted to take a real person who is featured only briefly in Scripture and find within her story meaning and hope for women everywhere. I have found myself identifying with Eve in ways that seemed ridiculous before. Now I wonder how I could ever look at her and not see pieces of myself.

God created her with a specific design. He did the same with me. He instilled in her all she would need to accomplish what she was created to do, but her weakness caused her to question those truths. I am guilty of the same. She was deceived because she was destined. So have I been deceived even while hearing God remind me of the great destiny He has for me. She failed in a moment though she knew God and had shown devotion to Him. How much like her I have been. I will tell the Lord I am thankful for how He made me and within moments of gazing in the mirror I will find negative things to say about my image. Eve's failures did not eliminate how creative and intricate she was made. Her decisions did not limit God's abilities. Nor do ours.

I never thought I had so much to learn from someone whose life is covered in only a handful of verses. But reading between the lines and listening for revelation from the Holy Spirit opened up doors to understanding that I never expected.

We are all small mirrors always being held up for everyone to see. Eve was not a saint, but she is a sister and a mother and a teacher to women like us who take the proverbial slide down the rabbit hole, lock eyes with evil, and answer the devil back. She is our ancient Alice in Wonderland, with time running out and a battle to win. As women lost or found we are all in our own wonderland experiences, and we need spiritual maturity to wake us up from the slumber of unbelief and move us in to reality.

Is it not the reality of our own lives that we need to maneuver well in? It is reality that enables us to connect. It is also reality that causes us to run and hide. Eve experienced real motives, real sin, real love, and real anguish and became a picture for us to look at. She became the model for the roles we all are tempted to play when we lose sight of who God made us to be.

Maybe the reason it has been hard for me to relate to Eve until now is that I thought more of her sin than her life. I allowed her sin to shape my view of her as woman instead of recognizing the intention of God in creating her first for the purpose of relationship. Shifting my perspective has changed everything.

As humans we were born unaware in our infancy of life's difficulties but engaged in the process of living. I learned love by the way my parents showed me love. That set inside me the need to parent with love. Eve was created without infancy but with God as her parent. God's love knit her together in His image outside of His being with the ability to conceive and procreate that same image. The humanity that God created out in open air would now be internally hand-stitched. Have you ever thought about this? I cannot help but ponder it.

Adam and Eve were not physically born; they were hand-crafted on the outside of God from His internal desire to fellowship with us. They were made with holy inspiration and invited to share in the deep of His heart and have relationship with Him. This would involve them entrusting the inner structure of their hearts to Him. Then He gave them the ability to produce what He had made, hoping they would do so with the same intention, devotion, and hope that He had in creating them.

Except this time instead of humanity being made with His hands outside the womb, as Adam and Eve were, the whole process would happen internally. Eve would birth a different way, producing the same human form, yet the process would take longer. Where God's idea manifested in a day, man's procreation would require months to develop.

This is a beautiful image not just of God's creative structure but also of His intensive plan to ultimately seat Himself on the inside of creation. A lost soul wanders outside of God's heart, and not until she finds salvation does she put away being lost and find the door in—the door to being found.

Revelation 3:20 paints the picture of Christ standing at the door of our hearts knocking and asking to be let in. How clever God was in creating this picture. God is not just the builder of the door of our hearts; He also is the one knocking to be let inside. He has thought of everything. But, of course, He is God—the One who commanded the womb to bear the image He created out of dust and bone over and over again. It is in this way that God's idea for redemption came into being—an idea birthed thousands of generations before one young girl would carry a Savior.

This does not make Eve just a baby maker. It makes her someone God entrusted to house what He creates. That sends chills up my spine. It speaks of her value and purpose in God's plan. We have been made with value and purpose too. Do you ever remind yourself of that, or do you constantly focus on your faults and weaknesses? Do you ever speak value and purpose over yourself? Words speak life or death, and the health of our souls and our belief in whose we are is incredibly important to our living this life well.

When we let the power of our words lower us to standards that expose us to an invasion of insults from the enemy, who loves to lie to us about our worth, we see only where our fault lines run. Surely we are not incapable of finding healing from the effects of these lies, or praying that healing in and over others! We are only incapable of healing if we become resistant to truth. Truth says we are fearfully and wonderfully made. Truth says where there is design, there is destiny.

When we find Eve, we find life inside her, and that life mirrors the beauty of God's trust. That trust reflects the degree of faith resident in her. How much do we desire faith? The answer will be different for each one of us.

Being Holy

Eve stood in the garden bold and beautiful, yet within a short period of time she would be convinced that she had nothing of value. Her guilt over her actions would have been enormous, and her resentment of herself would have given birth to the very insecurity we still fight today. I had to find this woman, who I knew I could understand beyond ancient walls and borders. Even though I was born so many millennia later, I still would take my place next to Eve, trying, like her, to figure out what was required of me in my day as a woman and a daughter of God.

When I consider Eve, I must consider how things have changed and then realize how so many things have not changed at all. Women fight the same battles she fought every day and bear the scars of Eve's unbelief. Is sin any different or disappointment any less messy in our day than it was in Eve's? Is marriage so much easier now than it was then? Is giving birth to a child any less painful? Does losing a child hurt any less? Does murder affect us differently now than it would have then? How can grief in any form be weighed from one era to another? This simply means we can relate to Eve, and there is so much to hope for in finding her.

I think of my relationship and devotion to this great God, and I still find myself a little envious of Eve. She heard God audibly. She knew Him on a deeper level than we can even imagine. I can only assume that in the end of her life, after walking with Him for so long, she was made more aware of God's divinity, and in seeing Him in eternity she would come face-to-face with His true holiness. It is often in the finality of our flesh that we submit fully to an eternal perspective.

I assume Eve had this same feeling as she came to the end of all she had known in her humanity and wrapped her heart around what she did not fully understand about eternity. When my own mother took her last breath, I watched the look on her face change from confusion to peace. I could see cancer lose the battle to heaven's arms, which were open and waiting to embrace her. Her last words were, "Look, my Messiah has come for me." She had worries, and she had concerns leaving six children who still needed her. Yet in those final moments, I watched as my mother let go of an understanding of this world to cling to a coming revelation of the next.

Eve was not so different. She had known through her failures what her life was supposed to look like. Maybe her final prayer was that those who came after her would do a better job of believing the truth and forsaking the lies.

The question can be asked then, is there personal purpose in finding Eve? Yes! We cannot disregard that even as humans we were made capable of being holy as He is holy (1 Pet. 1:15–17). Why would God invite us to share in His holiness if there were no hope of our being able to achieve it?

It is here that we must evaluate the pollution of unbelief that we may or may not be surrounded by and take note of what should or should not be growing in our own gardens.

We should consider the soil something important and rid the ground in our hearts of all that would keep good produce from growing there. We need not concern ourselves with the attention or approval of anyone but the Lord.

We need to raise the standards of holiness in our own lives and understand that grace is not staying surrounded by or stuck in our sin. Grace is red blood that ran down the body of a King bearing your sin so you could get free of it.

What does it mean to be holy? Being holy is not being addicted to substances or relationships other than those that are godly. It is not saying something is OK and God-centered when it is killing you inside and robbing you of self-respect. So many are still being met by a serpent near a tree in the garden of their lives and being persuaded to believe in a lie that has a death grip attached to it.

We are kidding ourselves if we think God is sitting on our couches watching half of what we have become so infatuated with on television. We can't say sin is OK because we don't want to be "religious." The enemy looks for every crack, and most of the ones you don't think he can fit into he has already used to gain access to your life.

Holiness isn't popular because religion has messed it up. It is right to realize that our relationship with God is not based on a list of dos and don'ts, but drawing a line in the sand does not make us religious. It is not religious to believe abortion is not a choice but the slaughtering of innocent lives. It is, however, religious to make someone who has gone through an abortion feel condemned and hopeless.

I mention abortion because it is the enemy's direct attempt to screw up one of Eve's purposes. She was born to birth life, not to kill it. To many people these days, purity seems overrated because the media has us more captivated than Scripture.

God loves the one committing the sin, but He will never love the sin. Addiction in any form is sin—period. Rebellion in any form is sin—period. Premarital sex is sin—period. Homosexuality is sin—period. Uncontrollable drinking and drug abuse is sin. Society may want us to believe otherwise, but only the truth will make people free.

We must have compassion in dealing with those who are struggling in these areas. The reason those who are stuck and confused don't want to listen to the message of the gospel is that they have never seen religion wear the godly coat of love. This is the fault of the church. We must be God's hands and feet. I've made mistakes, but God never told me I was a failure. He told me He could cause my failures to become my success *in Him*!

UNDOING THE DARKNESS

We can name all the ways our standards have been lowered and our ideas changed because we challenged God's Word or, like Eve, listened to the enemy's questions and let him plant doubt in our minds. I worry about this the most. There are so many things I was foolish enough to allow and not speak up and ask God about. God is so forgiving and lovely in His way of undoing the darkness we allow to shackle us.

There is a challenge, though, for the church when encouraging modern-day Eves to seek redemption from bondage. As sin becomes more popular and a lie more believable, women have a harder time finding true freedom as the lines are blurred. At times the world is shouting louder that darkness is OK than the church is shining the light of truth into that darkness. It seems the church as a whole is confused about what she believes is righteous and holy. If the bride does not know the boundary lines, how will she set them as a path for her children to follow?

I have had grace and compassion for the sinner, but I still hate the sin and what it does to the believer and the unbeliever. My grief is deeper for the saved who act as though they are lost than for the lost who behave the only way they have ever known to act—lost! I came into some friendships with people who had a God-centered mentality and found myself confused about issues I had always had a firm understanding of. I felt persuaded to think certain behaviors and beliefs were somehow insignificant or ridiculous to focus my attention on. Thankfully His mercy led me back to a place of truth and knowledge. There are many, though, who don't know where the boundary lines are anymore.

We can put ourselves in a place that slowly steers us away from the truth. If we stay there, we eventually will grow new ideas that are not rooted in godly foundations and become loyal to those wrong beliefs instead of the original truth that is in Scripture. God created boundary lines so that we wouldn't question what we should be loyal to. As women we need to set up more godly boundaries and stop allowing ourselves to be manipulated by what the culture or a popular pastor has to say. And we need to stop manipulating others with ungodly beliefs!

Eves today must be called back to their first love. The only way this can happen is if we are fully willing to face God's truth as real truth. There is no real peace outside of that. We must begin the weeping and the mourning as Rachel did (Jer. 31:15) for the loss of our children's inheritance.

It is unfair for me to think I could have done better if I had been Eve. I have too many regrets of my own to think so highly of myself. I have fallen and failed and listened to the serpent's lies. Yet it was in those failures that I found grace for Eve. In finding grace for her, I was able to call upon grace for my own life. I rose back up and set my sight on hope again and again. I was able to cry out and see my idols come crashing down and my self-esteem rise to match God's opinion of me.

The purpose in finding Eve here is to understand her from our shared emotions and our shared circumstances. She was real, and she experienced being a woman without any guidance, as she was the only one for a while. There is pressure in this, for sure, and it is a pressure that has passed on through generations. But it is a pressure that should become our pleasure. We still are one of a kind, and it is our right to enjoy being unique.

Yet instead of taking pleasure in our uniqueness, we doubt our worth and think we are not good enough. We question authority and find trusting God a long, uphill trek. We struggle to find contentment. We complain about our weight, look for youth in lotions and potions, and want to cut away the markers of time. We find consolation in what we can produce and how educated we become. We fight to climb ladders of corporate success. We desperately long not to be alone, wishing for greener pastures without understanding that a woman can be married and still feel alone.

The soul of every Eve longs for the same stability that God supplied there in that original garden. Because of distractions and low self-worth we struggle to reach it, but it is there nonetheless. It beckons us to keep reaching. Finding Eve—as a resource instead of a cautionary tale—may cause us to see that God gave us value there in the beginning, and it still is resident in us today.

We want more for our children, but we don't know how to first find healing for our own fractured hearts to avoid leaving behind a legacy of generational cursing. There is so much we can learn from Eve, but how do we change? I believe we cry out to God and call for Him to show us once again the simple beauty that He saw in His heart when He first created us. We can read the Word, identify all the freedom signs, and follow them. We can be devoted to Christ, get delivered of oppression, and become even more devoted to claim even more freedom.

We can accept what we have lost and stop regretting what we cannot reclaim. We can forgive and trust again. We can let go of the season of miscarriages and breakups, and return to the great Husband and Healer and lay down to find mercy at His feet. We can abide and hide under the shadow of His wings. We will pursue and prevail, persist and push through all that life tosses our way and still love and laugh and choose to live. That is the key to it all once again: choice.

If Eve knew then what would become of women and how her choices would cascade down through the ages, causing so many questions and such deep disturbance to God's original design, I am sure she would have tried harder. Daughters of Eve, can we not avoid making that mistake? Can we not love instead of hate? Can we not heal instead of harbor resentment? Can we not forgive instead of live in offense? Can we not encourage instead of deny affirmation? Can we not start living instead of simply surviving? Can we not walk out purpose and not live in regret? Can we not do all we can do to find wholeness and hope and fall into the arms of a loving God?

In searching for Eve, what I have found is more of God. I have found that He is still marvelous and miraculous in all He does, and I have discovered that He loves me more deeply than I could imagine love to be. I believe that I was made in secret and wonderfully crafted to live and breathe and make Him famous. He assigned my gender and had no intention of me being anything other than female. I was not a mistake. I am a miracle. I was not made to be alone; the aloneness I've felt has made me aware that He is always there. I was made to honor Him and not honor the world. In honoring what God made when He created me, I honor His hand and His plan and negate the right of the enemy to lie and say I am not enough.

Finding Eve has made me more aware of the strength I inherited from God to see a lie for what it is and not allow it to manipulate my future. Eve failed in that garden, but that does not mean her life was a complete failure. Her restoration can become our resurrection and our hope. God can be disappointed in our actions, but His nature is to always point to our future. I have great hope for all Eves today. I think we are worth believing in. I think we are worth encouraging.

Even though the stakes are high and the distractions are greater now, God is still in love with each one of us! I find Eve in me and my mother and my sisters. I am grateful, thankful, and amazed by the way God's love for her is still evident in me.

I am most thankful for God's ideas and His creative expression. He showed off when He created Eve. He showed off in making her beautiful and giving her the ability to bring forth life. He has continued to breed hope and a wealth of compassion deep inside Eves today, and to give us every opportunity to prosper in spirit and creativity! He does not hold us back but encourages us to set our hearts toward things above and believe for more to come.

I am an Eve. I was saved from the serpent that came calling to me by a love too great to fully comprehend. None of us deserve His salvation, but all of us can receive it. I am eternally thankful for this. Every morning mercy dances outside our windows. God stands back and knocks and waits for us to answer and invite Him in. He was a gentleman in the garden and a gentleman on the cross. His power is limitless, and His love flows regardless, yet He will not force His way into our hearts.

He is worth the risk we must take to trust Him. He is the soft shoulder we can cry on in our sorrow. He will see us safely into the future He has appointed for us. We must simply believe that we do, in fact, have a future. I penned a song recently, and the first line is my favorite: "I was not a flame, until You struck me with Your love; now I burn for You." We need to burn for Him, knowing that His heart is on fire for us.

Eve had a choice. Her decision changed us all. The good news is that we all have been given the same choice, and greatness comes when we choose well. Dear sisters, daughters, mothers, and wives, even if your own mothers and fathers knew nothing about God in your conception, even if there are a heap of troubles at your feet, you still can choose. You came into being for a reason, and there is a place for you at God's table.

The circumstance you face will challenge your faith, and you can make a million excuses for why you chose the lifestyle you have chosen or to believe what you believe. The truth is that one day every knee will bow to the One whose name is above every name (Phil. 2:10).

I am thankful for Eve and for Eden. I am thankful that God put a man to sleep and pulled out of him promise in the form of a rib. God thought of Eve in thinking of a way to house His Son, and then with His Son He pulled me, a daughter of Eve, back to His side. I am so thankful for Eve, that even in her failure she led me to His success. She has pointed to God and His deity. In finding Eve, I have found the Lord still to be everything He said He is, was, and ever will be. There is hope for this girl yet.

NOTES

Chapter 1
Finding an Education

1.   BibleStudyTools.com, s.v. "*racham*," http://www
.biblestudytools.com/lexicons/hebrew/nas/racham.html (accessed
February 4, 2013).

Chapter 7
Finding Influence

1.   As quoted in H. B. Pratt, Wm. C. Brown, C. Stone,
H. G. Park, editors, *The Mother's Assistant, Young Lady's Friend
and Family Manual* (Boston: Stone & Pratt, 1851). Viewed at
Google Books online.

Chapter 9
Finding Balance

1.   *Merriam-Webster's Collegiate Dictionary*, 11th edition
(Springfield, MA: Merriam-Webster, Inc., 2003), s.v. "balance."

Chapter 11
Finding Courage

1.   Dictionary.com, s.v. "courage," http://dictionary.reference
.com/browse/courage?s=t (accessed February 6, 2013).

ABOUT THE AUTHOR

Rita Springer is known for her unscripted, spontaneous style of worship. She has penned such favorites as "Make Us a Prayer," "You Are Still Holy," "Worth It All," and most recently "This Blood." Her voice is also known to cover such songs as "You Said" from Hillsong and Mercy Me's "I Can Only Imagine." She has recorded more than seven albums and has traveled the world leading and teaching worship and women's conferences.

Out of her music has grown a passion to mentor and empower women. In March 2008, Rita launched the DIVE Worship School. DIVE is an acronym for Deep Innovative Vertical Expression. This school is a one-week intensive training course for those with a gift in the cultural and creative arts. In this course Rita encourages her students in their creative gifts and equips them to go to deeper levels of freedom and greater heights of expression via a relationship with God.

Rita also began leading and teaching the Finding Eve conferences for women in 2010. These conferences came from a desire to see women set free and are partly what compelled Rita to write this book.

Rita resides in Colleyville, Texas, with her son, Justice, whom she adopted at birth. She enjoys being a mother and takes the responsibility of raising up the next generation seriously. Rita splits her time between traveling on the road and being on staff as a pastor in the worship ministry at Gateway Church in Southlake, Texas.

Rita would love to hear from you. Please connect with her at:

rita.springer@gatewaypeople.com
www.ritaspringer.com
Gateway Church
500 S. Nolen
Southlake, TX 76092
817-552-7474

If you would like to host a Finding Eve conference at your church, please e-mail findingeve@aol.com or visit the website at www.findingeve.org.

If you would like to apply for a DIVE Worship School, please apply at www.diveworship.com.

OTHER RESOURCES
BY RITA SPRINGER

The Playlist

Created to Worship

Worth It All

I Have to Believe

Effortless

Rise Up

Beautiful You

All I Have

To order Rita's resources, please visit her website at
www.ritaspringer.com or download her music at
iTunes - Music - Rita Springer
https://itunes.apple.com/us/artist/rita-springer/id7019177.